TAMING THE WRITING TIGER:

A Handbook for Business Writers

Second Edition

by

James L. Brimeyer

Writing Instructor

Northeast Iowa Community College

Uncial Press   **Aloha, Oregon**

2007

Taming the Writing Tiger, 2nd Edition, by James L. Brimeyer

ISBN-13: 978-1-60174-030-4
ISBN-10: 1-60174-030-1
Copyright © 2006, 2007 by James. L. Brimeyer
Published 2006. Second Edition 2007.

Published by Uncial Press
An imprint of GCT, Inc.
2550 SW 204th Ave.
Aloha, Oregon 97008

For online purchase, visit http://www.uncialpress.com

Printed in the United States of America.

Library of Congress Cataloging-in-Publication Data

Brimeyer, James L., 1947-
   Taming the writing tiger : a handbook for business writers / by James L. Brimeyer. — 2nd ed.
      p. cm.
   ISBN 978-1-60174-030-4 (pbk.)
   1. Business writing. 2. English language—Business English. I. Title.
   HF5718.3.B75 2007
   808'.0665—dc22
                              2007016706

This book is dedicated to:

My wife Kay, for her unending support and love
over the years

my family—Joe and Amy, Ellen; and grandchildren—
Mariah, Kayla, Evan—their grandpa's treasures

With thanks:
I thank Greg Burbach and Bob Donovan for their kind
endorsements which appear on the back cover of this book.

I also thank my wonderful publishing team—Judith B. Glad, Dick
Claassen, and Katie Struck—for their conscientious efforts,
creativity, and guidance in developing this book.

About the Author

Jim Brimeyer has taught writing courses at Northeast Iowa Community College since 1989. Before that, Jim taught high school English for 25 years. He received his BA and MA in English Education from Loras College in Dubuque, Iowa. Jim's college composition textbook, *You've Gotta' Have Heart in Your Writing*, is now in its second edition. Jim's booklet, *Response and Self-Reflection: the Heart and Soul of My Writing Classroom*, was published in 2002 by the Iowa Writing Project. Jim's articles have been published in NCTE's *Teaching English in the Two-Year College, The Successful Teacher, The Teaching Professor, Portfolio News, Iowa Language Arts News, and Julien's Journal*. Jim is actively involved in the Iowa Writing Project and serves as an instructor for IWP, in addition to his teaching at NICC. He has given countless pedagogical presentations from coast to coast.

Jim Brimeyer's honors include the ICTELA Iowa Literacy Award, the National Council of Instructional Administrators Award for Community College Teaching, the NISOD Teaching Excellence Award from the University of Texas at Austin, University of Notre Dame Educator Award, University of Chicago Outstanding Teacher Award, and the Iowa State University Excellence in Teaching Award. In 2005, Jim was selected Iowa Professor of the Year by the Carnegie Foundation for the Advancement of Teaching and the Council for Achievement and Support of Education. Jim was also named the 2006 Outstanding Community College Faculty Member by the Iowa Association of Community College Trustees.

Table of Contents

CHAPTER 1

Getting Down to Business—Writing

*The estimated cost of business communication in American
business and industry is more than $75 billion yearly. And
roughly 60 per cent of the writing is inefficient: unclear,
misleading, irrelevant, deceptive, or otherwise wasteful
of time and money"(5).* – John M. Lannon

In 2004, The National Commission on Writing conducted a
survey of the top 120 American corporations in order to study the quality
of writing among American salaried employees. The study revealed that
80 percent or more of salaried employees in the business sector are
expected to write as part of job performance. Furthermore, the National
Commission study emphasized the importance of good writing skills for
gaining employment, for performing written responsibilities on the job,
and for being considered for promotion. The study also found that major
American corporations are spending $3.1 billion annually to remediate
deficient writing among their employees (18).

Does this mean that writers in the business sector are
incompetent? Not at all. In fact, everyone, including business personnel,
can write and write well. But, like any skill, writing demands focused
attention and continuous practice. "Writing is a craft in which no one
becomes a master," commented Ernest Hemmingway. So corporations
and businesses should be commended for recognizing the importance of
quality writing and providing opportunities for employees to polish and
upgrade their writing skills.

Many employees would rather visit their dentist for root canal
work than tackle a writing assignment, however. Why do many
employees feel inadequate when it comes to writing? Some simply lack
confidence in their writing abilities. Others carry negative experiences
with writing from their schooling. Some business majors feel that their
undergraduate college experiences never prepared them for the extensive

writing demands of their jobs. Despite the multitude of reasons for the lack of writing confidence, all professional and business employees can write at the level of proficiency demanded of their jobs. Writing effectively does not require the artistry of Stephen King or J.K. Rowling. Many business writers simply need to become aware of the ingredients for clear, clean business writing and take the time to implement those ingredients. The ideas in this handbook are designed to provide business writers with easy-to-grasp "tricks of the trade" so that they can write clear, clean documents for any purpose and audience.

Clear, clean writing reflects your competence as a writer and employee. By the same token, poor writing decreases customers' confidence in you as an employee and in your organization. Any time you sign your name or use your company's logo, it is a reflection on both you and your company. Poor writing and editing may cause readers to question your intelligence or, even worse, your attitude and work ethic. Poorly written business communication destroys your individual credibility and that of your company.

> *"Write the way you speak and your writing will be*
> *much more lively, powerful and engaging than if*
> *you write the way you think writing should sound" (28).*
> —Richard Andersen and Helene Hinis

IDENTIFY THE AUDIENCE AND PURPOSE

Although this sounds like a given, business writers need to identify the audience, WHOM you are writing to. Also, identify the purpose of your correspondence—WHAT and WHY you are writing. It helps to provide the reason for your writing as early as possible in your letter. Your reader must understand your message and be motivated to accomplish your purpose. The correspondence should build your company's public relations and goodwill and enhance your personal reputation as a respected, knowledgeable employee.

Also, analyze your audience to determine how you will address your reader. Should you use his/her first name in a more informal tone, or should you address your reader by a formal title like Doctor, Professor, Mr., or Miss? If you are not sure of your reader's identity, research pertinent information. It only takes a couple of extra minutes to phone or check email to determine whether Chris Cross is Christopher or Christine. That couple of minutes could later save a couple hours, possible embarrassment, and a lost account.

Readers keep busy schedules, so write as concisely as possible. Let readers get in and get out of your correspondence. They do not have time to waste, and they appreciate terse, succinct, clear, clean writing that gets to the point. "Put up and shut up!" in business communication. Keep the writing short and clear—preferably one page.

Write in a conversational, respectful tone as if you are writing for and communicating with an intelligent friend. Try to give your readers a sense of recognition and personal importance. Also, try to write as clearly and simply as possible. Your readers may not have technical training in your area of expertise, so keep technical jargon out of the writing as much as possible. To address your audience in a more personal way, write in second person—you—and refer to yourself in first person—I, me. This less formal tone helps readers connect with you, the writer, as a real person. Avoid the stiff, formal third person—he, she, it, they, one, the reader—which establishes distance between the writer and the audience.

> YUK—It is hoped by this writer that Brim's Broom can be utilized by the reader to the utmost satisfaction.
>
> YES —I hope Brim's Broom serves your cleaning needs.

Your audience is a real human being, not a zombie from Mars, so write in a conversational tone—from intelligent friend to intelligent friend. Some writers try to impress readers by using multiple-syllabic words that make them sound more like "brainiacs" than real human beings. Rather than using brainiac verbage like, "Let's engage in a loquacious palaver," write in a personal, sincere voice by saying, "Let's visit." Word choices in business writing should focus on clear, concise communication. A pretentious vocabulary does not make good writing. Clear, concise, correct word choices make powerful writing. If a reader needs to consult a dictionary, you have used "brainiac verbage" rather than a conversational tone. Regarding "brainiac" word usage, Mark Twain offers all writers sage advice: "Never use five dollar word when a five cent one will do." Create a positive tone in your business correspondence by using the six C's of effective business writing:

**Courteous, Cordial, Conversational,
Clear, Concise, Correct.**

The best business communication is written in a conversational tone. Avoid trying to sound ultra upper crust by using brainiac phrases like:

In reference to your letter of...	Enclosed therewith please find...
Pursuant to our agreement...	As per our telephone conversation...
In accordance with your request...	To be perfectly honest...
Needless to say...	As you are aware...
Please rest assured...	Please be advised that...
At your earliest convenience...	For your perusal...

Finally, in business writing, you can't be wrong by using the KISS method:

Keep It Simple, Stella (Stan)!

PRACTICE 1A: Rewrite the following passages to clarify the brainiac word choices.

Passage 1   Mammals of the family Ursidae of the order Carnivora habitated the elements of the secondary xylem comprising the bulk of the stem of habitation produced by the Cambium. The social group consisted of the male begetter and sire, the bearer of the offspring, and the neonate of the paternal and maternal guardians. This triad of organisms of the family of the Kingdom Animala favored nourishment consisting of supawn oatmeal blended with a glandular secretion of the bovine genus.

Passage 2   Recent interlocutions with various personnel at all levels of the company have illuminated the fact that a prodigious, numerical quantity of office personnel are over-extending their scheduled daily intermissions. This is not pursuant to company policy and in non-conformance with the legal and binding contract. Therefore, be it duly noted that henceforth, all company personnel must return without tardiness to their assigned stations as soon as the quarter hour of elapsed intermission has subsided.

CHAPTER 2

Plan Your Work. Work Your Plan.

"0.8 percent of the human race is capable of writing
something that is instantly understandable" (15).
– H.L. Mencken in Zinnser

The Writing Process

Brainstorm/Plan
Pre-write   **Writer Focus**
Draft

Rewrite/Revise   **Reader Focus**
Edit

Brainstorming/Planning

Writers begin the brainstorming stage the second they begin to think about the writing assignment. Writers' brains immediately begin a mental search for ideas before they write anything on paper or type anything on a screen. This unlocking of the brain is natural and fruitful. You may think of writing ideas as you drive to and from home or work. You may even think of something for a writing purpose in your sleep. Or you may talk about your topic and ideas with family, friends, or associates and even choose to tape-record your conversation. Importantly, however, you must capture your thoughts so these ideas can't escape. This leads to the initial stage in the writing process—pre-writing.

Pre-writing

Once you have identified your purpose and audience, you prepare for the writing by capturing ideas on paper and by generating more ideas using pre-writing strategies, such as slash outline, formal outline, cluster, or fishbone. Getting started may present problems for some writers, and the more they think about the topic or assignment, the more pressure they feel. Pre-writing helps writers get started on paper. Pre-writing might be compared to loosening up your brain muscles so you can think freely about ideas and ways to gather them. The strategy you choose to pre-write will depend on your topic and your preference as the writer. No one strategy works best for all writers. The key is to unlock your brain, to generate as many ideas as possible about your topic, and to capture those ideas. Once you begin to write a draft, you may choose to use most of the ideas you generate or choose to dispose of some that don't seem to fit. In addition, you may add or delete ideas once you begin the drafting itself. In prewriting, you might use one of the following:

✔ *Slash Outline*

Autobiography

In using a slash outline, you simply list every idea that comes into your brain about your topic. By writing ideas on paper, you may generate as many ideas as possible and gain control of your topic so that you don't later forget good ideas you initially generated.

birth
family
school
jobs
marriage
hobbies
future plans

✔ *Formal Outline*

Some writers choose the formal outline because they have worked with it in their earlier school experiences. By using Roman numerals, letters, and numbers, writers generate ideas while beginning to organize these ideas at the same time. This pre-writing strategy works for some. However, many writers find that its formal structure doesn't allow the flexibility and freedom of other pre-writing strategies. But if a formal outline works for you, use it.

AUTOBIOGRAPHY

I. Birth
   A. Mercy Hospital
   B. July 19, 1947
   C. Family
      1. Leon Brimeyer
      2. Grace Link
      3. Brother - Rick

II. Education
   A. Elementary - Buenie & Holy Ghost
   B. High School – Wahlert
   C. College – Loras
   D. Post-college – Loras, Iowa, Iowa State, UNI, Carleton

III. Employment
  A. Teen – newspaper carrier,
      Grocery delivery
  B. College - music-Shakey's; TH
      sports writer, Ref FB & BB

IV. Marriage
  A. Kay
  B. Kids – Joe & Ellen

V. Hobbies
  A. Reading
  B. Golf
  C. Walking
  D. Watch sports

VI. Plans
  A. Enjoy teaching and life
  B. Book

✔   *Cluster (Web or Mind-map)*

The cluster, also called web or mind-map, allows writers to generate ideas that expand like a growing bush. Place your topic in the middle of your page and write every idea that your brain generates as off-shoots of the topic. This strategy also allows your brain to begin to organize ideas into sections or clusters. As writers see where their brain takes them in generating ideas, they are subconsciously stimulated to expand on ideas that fit into each section or cluster.

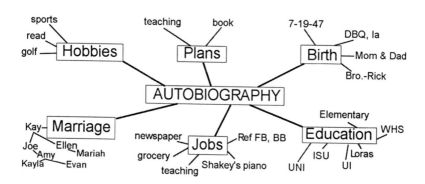

✔   *Fishbone*

The fishbone resembles the cluster, but takes a lateral format. Place your topic on the left side of your paper. Then on a lateral line, write every idea that your brain generates about your topic.

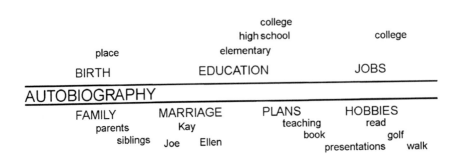

Writers have used other pre-writing strategies than these. From your previous writing experiences, you may have developed a different pre-writing strategy, which helps you unlock your brain. Don't re-invent the wheel. Use what works for you and gives you confidence. You may want to experiment with other pre-writing strategies to see which one will work best for you in different writing situations. Also, note that you are not restricted to using just one pre-writing strategy. Maybe more than one will help generate even more ideas.

"Writing is rewriting what has already been rewritten" (195).
— Elizabeth Danziger

Drafting/Writing

Once you feel you have given enough time to generating ideas through pre-writing, you will need to move to the keyboard or take up your pen to begin drafting. You will use ideas you generated with your pre-writing strategies to help you compose. As you write, you may add ideas as they come to you. Most importantly in this drafting stage of the process, write from your heart. Let your words and ideas flow freely onto the paper. Write freely and naturally. You are using this drafting stage to begin to formulate your piece of writing, not to finalize it. So let it happen. Don't worry about organization, sentence structure, word choice, usage, spelling, or punctuation. Get your ideas onto the page. Many times writer's block occurs because writers try too hard to get it correct the first time. They worry more about correcting their writing than creating their writing, causing them to block the flow of ideas. So let the ideas flow from your heart. You can attend to correctness in the editing stage. Also, don't worry about that splendid introduction to grab your readers' attention and keep them engaged. You can return to that part of the writing later after you see where your drafting takes you.

"Revising a document is like sanding a piece of furniture. You sand the wood for a while and then check to see if it is smooth yet. You sense a few bumps or rough edges, so you sand it some more. You check it again and sand it again, over and over until the wood looks and feels right. Similarly, you revise your document over and over until the whole thing flows smoothly" (196).
— Elizabeth Danziger.

Revising/Rewriting

After you have written your draft, you are ready to move to the next stage, revision. As the word RE-VISION suggests, with your readers in mind, you will take another look at your writing, another "vision," to see how you might develop and improve the piece, to take it forward. During this revision stage, the focus remains on ideas, content, organization, tone, and vocabulary which can enhance your writing. During the revision stage, you might add or delete ideas, rearrange them, provide more details or examples; do anything that might clarify and strengthen your piece. At this point in the process, do not worry about editing correctness. That step will come. Revise to focus on the clear meaning and organization of your text.

Throughout your process, keep in mind the advice of writer and teacher Joseph Williams, who says, "We write and revise our earliest drafts to discover and express what we mean, but in drafts thereafter, we write and revise to make it clear to our readers. At the heart of the process is the principle whose model you probably recall: Write for others as you would have others write for you" (220).

"Make it perfect. No typos, no misspellings, no factual errors. If you're sloppy and let mistakes slip by, the person reading your letter will think you don't know better or don't care."
—Malcolm Forbes

Editing

At some point, you will need to focus on correctness to assist your audience in reading clearly and easily. In this stage, you will check not only the clarity of your ideas but also your sentence development, correct word choice, grammatical usage, spelling, capitalization, and punctuation. You might wish to use a few techniques which work well during the editing stage.

First, read your piece aloud. This allows you to "plug in" two extra senses – speaking and hearing – to help clarify and clean your writing. Many times you will feel, see, sense, and catch areas of your writing that don't sound right or don't feel right or don't look right. Then you can make necessary changes. You might also consider reading your piece of writing into an audio tape-recorder and playing it back. Many times you will hear what sounds out of place or choppy or incorrect. Then you can adjust or fix those areas.

Second, read your piece of writing in reverse. Start with the last sentence of the piece and work your way backward to the beginning. This helps you isolate each individual sentence, and you can correct it separately for meaning, plus usage, spelling, punctuation, and the like. When you read from the beginning to the conclusion in natural order, your brain tends to focus on ideas because it naturally knows what you have written and jumps ahead looking for those ideas. You then may miss the cosmetic features of your writing that make it correct and easier to read.

Third, get an editor. Find a colleague(s) or administrative assistant(s), anyone (the more the merrier) whom you trust to help you improve your piece of writing. Then be open to suggestions and changes. The more responses and reactions you get from others, the better you will sense what works and does not work in your writing. Then you can make necessary revisions and corrections.

Finally, always use the advantage of technology, which offers spell-check programs and grammar checkers built into computer programs. However, remember that the spell checker will not catch every misspelled word. It will not be able to distinguish homonyms and recognize the difference between its-it's, your-you're, there-their-they're, to-two-too, etc. And your grammar checker may locate but not distinguish between correct word usage, such as good vs. well, or pronoun cases, for example.

> *"During an episode of Prairie Home Companion,*
> *Garrison Keilor once introduced a dog that growled*
> *every time he heard a grammatical error. In real life, unfortunately,*
> *most business people and professionals must become their*
> *own watchdogs and growl at their own work. The ability to correct*
> *one's own mistakes—to catch the culprits, so to speak—could be*
> *the difference between retaining or losing a client, a grant or even a job."*
> —Lynne Agress

PRACTICE 2A: Develop a full process—pre-write, draft, revision, and edited draft—for the following topic:

Explain your position at your place of employment, your length of employment with this company, and the specific duties your position requires. Explain any professional training that has prepared you for the job—formal education, job training, previous jobs. In addition, explain what kinds and how much writing your present position requires. You may address these ideas in any organized order, and you may add any pertinent information. Support your ideas by editing carefully for clarity, paragraph development, sentence structure, usage, spelling, capitalization, and punctuation.

CHAPTER 3

Structure Your Correspondence

Business Writing
Establish Goodwill

A little bit of QUALITY
will always make 'em smile:
A little bit of COURTESY
will bring 'em in by the mile;
A little bit of FRIENDLINESS
will tickle 'em, 'tis plain—
And a little bit of SERVICE
will bring 'em back again.

STRUCTURE of BUSINESS LETTERS: OPENING, MIDDLE, CLOSING PARAGRAPHS

Writers may use any number of strategies to capture readers' attention in the opening paragraph, maintain that attention throughout the body of support and evidence, and bring closure to the correspondence. Ineffective writing of any of these parts may cause readers to feel disjointed, disappointed, or disillusioned. An interesting opening lures readers into the letter while an effective closing ushers readers out, hopefully with more knowledge and insight than before reading the letter.

"A lead should be provocative. It should
have energy, excitement, an implicit promise
that something is going to happen or that some
interesting information will be revealed. It should
create curiosity, get the reader asking questions"(33).
–Gary Provost

OPENING PARAGRAPH

A courteous, cordial, concerned tone in the beginning paragraph engages readers and urges them to continue reading. Besides setting the tone, the opening announces and limits your subject, indicates an organization for the essay, and establishes a point of view that will accomplish your purpose. The opening of the correspondence gives the reader an impression of what will follow and urges the reader to read on. On the other hand, a dull, boring beginning can make readers stop immediately. Note, often the opening paragraph may be written after the body of the letter is developed since later paragraphs or the finish of the letter may suggest an effective opening.

In business writing, the opening paragraph should be should short, simple, and to the point and should establish good will. It should be written in a courteous, cordial, concerned tone.

Examples:

> We want to welcome you to the Two Teeth Comb Company and tell you how pleased we are to have you as our customer. We have received your order for four dozen of our new "Jumbo Nuclear Feel" combs. They should arrive within three working days.

> We at Two Teeth Company are delighted to have this opportunity to serve you. Your order of four dozen of our new "Jumbo Nuclear Feel" combs should arrive within three working days.

> Thank you for sending us the six defective "Jumbo Nuclear Feel" combs. We at Two Teeth Company agree that the quality of those six items is not up to our usual standard of excellence. We will replace them immediately, and you should receive the new shipment within three working days.

MIDDLE PARAGRAPHS

> *"A lot of nonsense has been written in writing textbooks about paragraphs, much of it not only wrong but harmful. Much of the nonsense arises from the false notion that every paragraph should*

be a short essay and that the thesis for the essay
should be expressed in something called a topic
sentence" (90). –Richard Marius

After you have gotten readers engaged via your opening, you need to keep them reading into the middle, or body, paragraphs of the correspondence, which support, develop, or prove your purpose. Writers develop the middle, supporting paragraphs to provide evidence through such strategies as examples, arguments, statistics, or quotations from authorities. Paragraph indentations signal changes to readers. A writer may indent to shift to new incident or supporting piece of evidence, to a different idea or a different slant, or maybe to restate or emphasize an idea. Paragraphing indentations usually occur naturally rather than accommodating the "old formula" of requiring a topic sentence and supporting sentences because "a paragraph is a miniature essay with a beginning, middle, and end." In fact, in her book, <u>A Rhetoric for Writing Teachers</u>, Erika Lindemann states that researchers found topic sentences in paragraphs "only 13% of the time" (152).

Rather than fitting paragraphs into the "old formula" of topic sentence followed by a specified number of supporting sentences, consider developing the length and depth of your paragraphs for reading ease. Write paragraphs that do not exceed eight lines of text. Long, rambling paragraphs cause readers to lose focus. Sometimes a special purpose, such as dialogue or emphasis, may call for even shorter paragraphs than the suggested eight lines of text. In <u>Writing With Style</u>, John R. Trimble suggests that paragraphing properly requires audience awareness and common sense rather than a formula. "Long paragraphs send off alarms in most readers' minds; very short paragraphs suggest insubstantiality and flightiness; a long succession of medium-length paragraphs indicates no imagination and proves monotonous. Moral: vary your pacing to keep your piece alive and vital" (81).

Paragraphing helps writers put order to their thoughts and break down ideas into manageable units. For readers, paragraphs make writing easier to follow, provide relief for the readers' eyes, and give readers confidence that they can absorb the piece one smaller block at a time. Consider indenting a new paragraph when a shift takes place for a: (1) change in emphasis or ideas, (2) change in time, (3) change in speakers, (4) change in place or setting. For clarity in paragraphs, use specific nouns early in each paragraph as antecedents for later pronouns, and avoid using vague nouns (a person, people) and pronouns (one, you, he, she, it, they). Also, maintain consistency in verb tense (present, past), person (first, second, third), and number (singular, plural).

Writers should consider two aspects of paragraphing, unity and coherence, in developing their paragraphs. Unity suggests that all ideas and sentences in a paragraph deal with the same idea or topic. Some writers use a "fishhook" technique to ensure unity. Each paragraph "fishhooks" into the thesis, and each paragraph "fishhooks" into the preceding and succeeding paragraphs. And each sentence "fishhooks" into the sentence before it and after it. Coherence implies a smooth, clear flow from idea to idea, sentence to sentence, and paragraph to paragraph. Most of the time, coherence happens naturally as writers use transitional words or repeat words or ideas as a means of flow.

However, a pattern of short, choppy sentences that seem to lack smooth flow could indicate a coherence problem stemming from a lack of transitions. To improve smoothness and transitions, a writer may repeat key words, use homonyms, use a pronoun referring to a preceding noun, or provide transitional words. The following chart of transitional words gives readers directional signals to help provide coherence in a piece of writing. But remember: don't overuse transitional words. Readers naturally sense changes and look for them in writing.

TRANSITIONAL CHART

Addition:	also, and, besides, finally, further, furthermore, in addition, likewise, moreover, then, too
Compare:	also, as well, in like manner, in the same way, likewise, similarly
Contrast:	although, but, despite, even though, however, nevertheless, still, on the contrary, on the other hand, otherwise, yet
Exemplification:	for example, for instance, in fact, in other words, specifically, that is
Place:	above, adjacent to, behind, below, beyond, close by, far, here, in front of, near, nearby, next to, north (south, east, west) of, on one side, opposite to, over, surrounding, through, within
Purpose:	to this end, for this purpose, with this object,
Result:	accordingly, as a result, because, consequently, for this reason, so, then, therefore,
Summary	and so, finally, in brief, in short, therefore,
Time:	after, afterward, at the same time, before, between, earlier, formerly, gradually, in the future, in the past, later, longer, meanwhile, now, since, soon, suddenly, then

CLOSING PARAGRAPH

*"Sum it up and get out. The last paragraph should tell
readers <u>exactly</u> what you want them to do—or what
you're going to do. Short and sweet."*
—Malcolm Forbes

The closing paragraph should bring closure to your correspondence and leave the reader with a satisfying, final impression. It reminds readers of your main point and hopefully gives them something to think about. The conclusion may even offer a recommendation or make a call to action. The conclusion may seem like a dog chasing its tail since it should relate to or connect to the opening or thesis without restating it. The opening and closing paragraphs frame the piece of writing.

The best closings display the same qualities as strong openings; they are simple and direct and written in a courteous, cordial, concerned tone.

Examples:

Please contact us at the Two Teeth Comb Company at any time if we can be of further service.

We at the Two Teeth Comb Company appreciate your business and hope we can serve you again soon.

In addition, if the conclusion suggests further action by the reader, make the date, action, and response as specific as possible. For example, instead of writing, "Please respond as soon as possible," or "Please call at your earliest convenience," write, "I look forward to hearing from you by phone (563.556.1234) by Tuesday at 10 AM." Ask your readers to respond to your request quickly. The longer readers are given to respond, the better the chance they won't.

Example:

YUK – I'll contact you when I get a chance.
YES – I will contact you at your office by phone by Tuesday noon to set up an appointment. I look forward to showing you the excellent service The Two Teeth Comb Company can provide.

Close your correspondence with a courteous word(s) such as:

Sincerely,   Cordially,   Best regards,   Yours truly,

Note that a comma follows the closing and only the first word is capitalized.

PRACTICE 3A: Create an effective business writing opening sentence and closing sentence that establish goodwill and are written in a courteous, cordial, concerned tone.

SAMPLE LETTERS

BLOCK STYLE LETTER

<table>
<tr><td>Brim's Writing Seminars
2436 Jupiter Lane
North Buena Vista, Iowa 52066</td><td>**Letterhead**</td></tr>
</table>

(2 spaces)

July 19, 2007   **Date**

(2 − 5)

Mr. Waldo Letterman
Shane Printing Company   **Inside**
360 Envelope Drive   **Address**
Wet Stamp, IA 54321

(2)

Dear Mr. Letterman: **Salutation**

(2)

Subject: Form of Block Letter   <u>Optional</u>

(2)

Thank you for attending last week's Brim's Writing Seminar and for your
recent request for information about letter writing format. This letter will
explain the block style business letter, which should consist of a minimum of   **Opening**
three paragraphs. Every line of the letter begins at the left margin. The first
paragraph should include a greeting and the purpose of the letter.

(2)

The middle section will consist of a paragraph(s) of details which specify the
who? what? when? where? and why? as they apply to the situation you are
writing about. You should write business correspondence in a conversational
tone focused on the personal importance of your reader(s). You are trying to   **Body**
enhance your company's public relations and build your own reputation as an
employee of merit. Sentences should average between 15 and 20 words, and
paragraphs should not exceed eight word-processed lines.

(2)

The final paragraph should provide a closing that will ensure goodwill. If you
desire certain action, you should suggest it before closing. This final paragraph
will also provide a friendly, positive farewell. If you have any further   **Conclusion**
questions, please contact me by noon on July 25, 2007, either by phone
(362.746.5432) or via e-mail at jbrim@coldmail.com.

(2)

Sincerely,   **Closing**

(2)

BRIM'S WRITING SEMINARS

(4)

Jim Brimeyer   **Signature**
Seminar Presenter

(2)

JB/kf   **References**

MODIFIED BLOCK STYLE LETTER
(With Indented Paragraphs)

Brim's Writing Seminars   **Letterhead**
2436 Jupiter Lane
North Buena Vista, Iowa 52066

(2 spaces)

          July 19, 2007   **Date**

(2 - 5)
Mr. Waldo Letterman
Shane Printing Company   **Inside**
360 Envelope Drive   **Address**
Wet Stamp, IA 54321

(2)
Dear Mr. Letterman: **Salutation**

(2)
Subject: Form of Block Letter   **Optional**

(2)
     Thank you for attending last week's Brim's Writing Seminar and
for your recent request for information about letter writing format. This
letter will explain the modified block style business letter, which should   **Opening**
consist of a minimum of three paragraphs. Every paragraph should be
indented. The first paragraph should include a greeting and the purpose
of the letter.

(2)
     The middle section will consist of a paragraph(s) of details which
specify the who? what? when? where? and why? as they apply to the
situation you are writing about. You should write business
correspondence in a conversational tone focused on the personal
importance of your reader(s). You are trying to enhance your company's   **Body**
public relations and build your own reputation as an employee of merit.
Sentences should average between 15 and 20 words, and paragraphs
should not exceed eight word-processed lines.

(2)
     The final paragraph should provide a closing that will ensure
goodwill. If you desire certain action, you should suggest it before
closing. This final paragraph will also provide a friendly, positive farewell.   **Conclusion**
If you have any further questions, please contact me by noon on July 25,
2007, either by phone (362.746.5432)) or via e-mail at
jbrim@coldmail.com.

(2)
          Sincerely,   **Closing**

(2)
       BRIM'S WRITING SEMINARS

(4)
         Jim Brimeyer   **Signature**
       Seminar Presenter

(2)
  JB/kf   **References**

PRACTICE 3B: Please create a letter based on the following prompt. Edit carefully for conciseness, sentence structure, usage, spelling, capitalization, and punctuation.

Prompt: Mr. U. R. Gladman, a manager of a local truck company and a long-time client, received his monthly billing last week for services provided by your company. His monthly bill is $9,164. But a miscalculation error billed his company $19,164. Therefore, your company owes Mr. Gladman $10,000. Please write a letter to Mr. Gladman informing him how the error was discovered, how the error occurred, and how the error will be rectified.

CHAPTER 4

Netiquette

"Composing email may not feel like writing. But it is writing, and it deserves the care you would put into any written work. The good news is that you can make your message as clear as possible before you send it. The bad news is that computer messages go everywhere instantly and then stick around forever" (222).
— Elizabeth Danziger

ln: rtd from nyc—☺ got your mail. tnx. yiu u want a f2f meeting this week; cnot. cldr is full. aamof, booked ntl feb. call 4 appt when u can. cul. jlb

Can you translate the preceding email message? Although it may save the writer/sender time, it will undoubtedly upset the receiver who has to decipher the message. Or probably, the receiver will just discard it as a foreign language. This type of email correspondence is inappropriate and unprofessional for business writing as well as personal correspondence. Email should be written as clearly, correctly, and courteously as any other business communication. Use the same approach to writing an email correspondence as you would in writing a paper copy letter. Plan your message, write it, and edit it. Remember you are sending the message to a live person on the receiving end, not to a translating machine.

Use the subject line under the address to grab your readers' attention. In email writing, the subject line serves the same purpose as a headline in a news article or a title of an essay. Therefore, your audience may or may not read your correspondence based on the effectiveness of your subject line. So try to capture the heart of your message in the subject line.

Since it is harder to read a computer screen than a letter on paper, keep your email short. As a courtesy to your reader, reduce the number of sentences in each paragraph, and reduce the number of words per sentence. Limit your line length to 65 characters. Consider using lists and bulleted items that are easier to read on the computer screen. Edit carefully for correct sentence structure, usage, spelling, capitalization, and punctuation. Avoid using abbreviations like those in the message at the beginning of this chapter. Like any business communication, email reflects on your company and you as an employee. So make it courteous, clear, and clean.

Avoid using *emoticons* like *smileys* ☺ or letter abbreviations (aamof– as a matter of fact) in business emails. They are disconcerting and unprofessional. Use standard English formation of capital and small letters. DO NOT WRITE YOUR MESSAGE IN ALL CAPITAL LETTERS. All capital letters in email jargon suggests you are screaming or shouting. Conversely, do not write your message in all small letters, which suggests you lack conviction.

- Avoid abbreviations (like the opening example).

b/c – because	imho – in my humble opinion
btw – by the way	lol – laugh outloud
fyi – for your information	rsn – real soon now

- Avoid emoticons:

Grin	\<g\>	Sigh	\<s\>
Just kidding	\<jk\>	Surprised	:-o
Lips are sealed	:-#	Tongue in cheek	:-J
Not funny	:/		

Finally, remember that the internet is not always secure, and privacy is never guaranteed. So always think what the results could be before you send an email. Make yourself look good in email correspondence because your message can be forwarded to anyone. Never write something you will later regret.

PRACTICE 4A: For the fun of it ☺, try to translate the passage at the beginning of this chapter.

CHAPTER 5

Strong Sentence Structure

*"The skills of new college graduates are deplorable—across the board;
spelling, grammar, sentence structure...I can't believe people come out
of college now not knowing what a sentence is" (14).*
–The National Commission on Writing

TIPS FOR WRITING SENTENCES

1. Write business sentences in a conversational tone.
2. "Less is more. The 'lean' style is in!" **Limit business writing sentences to between 15 and 20 words.**
3. Use a variety of long and short sentences.
4. Connect each sentence to the one before it and the one after it for smooth flow and continuity.
5. Vary sentence beginnings for variety.
6. Avoid beginning sentences with dummy subjects—There, Here, It.
7. Write sentences with nouns and verbs. Keep adjectives to a minimum, and use adverbs sparingly.
8. Don't write more than one dependent clause in a sentence, and don't put a dependent clause in every sentence.

DEAD SENTENCES: Fragments and Run-ons

SENTENCE FRAGMENTS

Sentence fragments, incomplete sentences, can confuse your readers and cause them to consider you a careless writer. So, edit carefully to insure that all sentences are complete, unless you write a fragment for a particular purpose.

Analyze the following types of fragments, grammatically incomplete sentences:

1. When the CEO finished reading the letter.
2. Hunting for his glasses.
3. Who talks in someone else's sleep.
4. The composition instructor on fourth floor.
5. At the top of the stairs to your left.

1. Number one, a dependent (subordinate) clause fragment, may be revised into sentences like,

   a. The CEO finished reading the letter.
   b. When the CEO finished reading the letter, she was delighted with the improvement in clarity.

2. Number two, a verbal (participle) fragment, might be revised into a sentence like,

   The professor's research work consisted of hunting for his glasses.

3. Number three, a relative clause fragment, might be revised into a sentence like,

   At times, professors talk in someone else's sleep.

4. Number four, a phrase fragment, might be revised into a sentence like,

   The composition instructor on the fourth floor has mastered the art of responding to students' writing.

5. Number five, a prepositional phrase fragment, might be revised into a sentence like,

   You will find your composition instructor at the top of the stairs and to the left.

THREE WAYS TO FIX FRAGMENTS:

1. **Add** words: Frag: More gas in Glen than in his car.
   Sentence: Glen stores more gas in his stomach than in his car.

2. **Delete** words: Frag: When Frank finished revising his business letter.
   Sentence: Frank finished revising his business letter.

3. **Hook** fragment to a nearby sentence:
   Frag: After I hit my head on the sidewalk.
   The cement cracked.

Sentence: After I hit my head on the sidewalk, the cement cracked.

Sentence: The cement cracked after I hit my head on the sidewalk.

Note: If the fragmented element comes before the sentence, a comma is needed after the fragmented element. However, usually no comma is required if the sentence precedes the fragmented element.

PRACTICE 5A: Editing Fragments   Correct the fragments in the following items.

1. Having already received five writing awards.

2. When I was in college. I found writing assignments easy. Mostly because of the simple topics which could be completed effortlessly.

3. Every day I drive 30 miles to work. Which becomes a hassle because of the increasing gas prices.

4. Although I fear business writing because I struggle with thinking of ideas to write about.

5. Through this writing seminar, I hope to increase my thinking skills. Both in generating ideas and in organizing them.

6. Although, with the job came many opportunities to write.

7. I am in the middle of my professional career. A career that I still look forward to.

8. College professors should require writing in all courses. From first semester through graduation.

9. Writing skills are developed with practice. And a willingness to learn new editing skills.

10. Business writing, which is much different from college, academic writing.

RUN-ON SENTENCES

A run-on contains two or more sentences punctuated as one sentence. Like fragments, run-ons can confuse readers and leave the impression of careless editing. Two kinds of run-ons are the fused sentence with no punctuation between sentences or the comma splice with only a comma between two sentences.

Fused: Waldo had served his company well he was given a raise.

Comma Splice: Waldo had served his company well, he was given a raise. *OR*
Waldo had served his company well, consequently he was given a raise.

FIVE WAYS TO FIX RUN-ONS:

1. **Compound Sentence:** add a comma and coordinating conjunction (For, And, Nor, But, Or, Yet, So = FANBOYS).
   Waldo had served his company well, and he was given a raise.

2. **Compound Sentence:** separate sentences with a semi-colon.
   Waldo had served his company well; he was given a raise.
   Waldo had served his company well; consequently, he was given a raise.

3. **Complex Sentence:** turn one into a dependent clause.
   Because Waldo had served his company well, he was given a raise.
   Waldo was given a raise because he had served his company well.

4. **Simple Sentence:** use a double verb.
   Waldo had served his company well and was given a raise.

5. **Simple Sentences:** separate sentences with a period.
   Waldo had served his company well. He was given a raise.

PRACTICE 5B: Editing Run-ons. Correct the run-ons in the following sentences.

1. I was recognized as a good writer, however I had little ambition to write.
2. Revision has always challenged me, I have always struggled with proper grammar.
3. I love to write I find it an interesting and rewarding mental challenge.
4. College professors told me I have writing talent I just detest spending so much time on one project.
5. Sharing my writing with my colleagues scares me they might find many errors and I might feel humiliated.

6. Writing is a skill or craft, it can be learned by everyone.
7. I took business writing four times in college unfortunately it was the same course four times.
8. I have lived in the same city all my life, I have worked as an insurance agent for ten years.
9. I have been promoted to Assistant Manager my supervisors recognized my hard work and positive attitude.
10. My confidence is soaring, I can't wait to write my next business communication.

PRACTICE 5C: Editing Fragments and Run-ons. Rewrite the following passage to eliminate the fragments and run-ons.

An eighty-eight-year-old lady could not find her favorite matching necklace and earrings. She searched every inch of her home. But she could not find her treasured jewelry. Her son, a lawyer of some renown. He advised his mother to file a claim with her insurance company. After giving her son's advice much thought. She chose to file the claim. And called her insurance agent. Obligingly, the service-oriented agent sent the lady the required forms. To apply for payment for her lost jewelry.

Upon receipt of the forms, she asked her son to help her fill them out. Which he dutifully did. The elderly lady then sent the claims to her agent, he filed them immediately the process to get the value of the jewels was put in motion. The insurance company sent the lady a check for $1,800 to cover the value of her missing gems.

A few weeks after receiving the check from the insurance company. The lady ran into her insurance agent at a super-market. Informed him that she had found her missing jewels in a box in her garage. The agent told her how pleased he was that she had located her treasured jewelry. And asked her to return the $1,800 to the insurance company.

The lady informed the agent that she could not return the money. When she found the jewelry. She felt it would not be fair to keep both jewels and money. So she put the $1,800 into the collection plate at her church.

PRACTICE 5D: Please create a letter based on the following prompt. Edit carefully for conciseness, sentence structure, usage, spelling, capitalization, and punctuation.

Prompt: Mr. I. M. Moody, a store owner and long-time client of your company, received his monthly bill from your company for services provided. In reviewing his bill, your accountant found that Mr. Moody's store was billed $725.40, when, in fact, the charges were actually $7,254.00 Please write a letter to Mr. Moody informing him how the error was discovered, how the error occurred, and how the situation will be rectified.

CHAPTER 6

Smooth and Clear: Parallelism & Misplaced, Dangling, Squinting Modifiers

*"Parallelism not only holds sentences together,
it adds emphasis, provides flow, expresses thoughts
more clearly, makes reading more pleasurable,
takes up less space, and makes what we say easy
to remember" (74).*
—Richard Andersen & Helene Hinnis

PARALLELISM

Parallel Structure in writing means using the same grammatical forms when writing pairs or a series (list of three or more items). Words are paired with words, phrases with phrases, and clauses with clauses. Parallel structure can add rhythm, style, grace, and power to your writing. Parallel structure may help you clearly express ideas of equal importance, highlight a comparison, or emphasize important ideas. Lack of parallel structure, on the other hand, makes writing sound choppy and disconnected. For example, note how two great craftsmen of literature use parallelism for emphasis and smooth flow. Charles Dickens begins *A Tale of Two Cities*, "It was the best of time, it was the worst of times, it was the age of wisdom, it was the age of foolishness..." William Shakespeare's Hamlet rhythmically states, "To die, to sleep. To sleep, perchance to dream" (3.1.55-56).

Note the breakdown of parallel structure in the following examples:

1. Alfred looks like a <u>miser</u>, an <u>egotist</u>, and <u>not married to a wife</u>.
            (noun)   *(noun)*   *(verb phrase)*

2. Hilda looks <u>healthy</u>, <u>wealthy</u>, and <u>an athlete</u>.
            (adj.)   *(adj.)*   *(noun)*

3. Old beliefs about witches have been rejected as <u>superstitions</u> and <u>detrimental</u> to society.   *(noun)*
  (adj.)

4. Irma was known as a <u>mother</u>, <u>married</u>, and <u>sewed</u> clothes.
                        (noun)   *(adj.)*   *(verb phrase)*

5. I love writing <u>for personal enlightenment</u> and <u>to develop mental creativity</u>.   *(prep. phrase)*   *(infinitive phrase)*

6. Mildred <u>not only</u> returned Homer's engagement ring <u>but also</u> his love letters were burned by her.   *(correlative conj.)*

Balance sentence structure, meaning, and rhythm by using the following suggestions for parallel structure:

A. **Use similar grammatical forms for items in pairs or in a series.**
   1. Minnesota Fats stands five feet two inches tall, a plump figure, and a weight of 238.
   ◆   Minnesota Fats stands 5'2", has a pump figure, and weighs 238 pounds.
   2. The sky looks pleasant and with no clouds in it.
   ◆   The sky looks pleasant and clear.
   3. Abigail likes to sing, dance, and to eat.
   ◆   Abigail likes to sing, dance, and eat. OR
       Abigail likes to sing, to dance, and to eat.

B. **Use similar grammatical forms in comparisons.**
   1. I like croquet better than to play indoors.
   ◆   I like croquet better than indoor games.

C. **Use the same grammatical forms for subject and predicate nominative.**
   1. To see is believing.
   ◆   Seeing is believing. *OR* To see is to believe.

D. **Use the same grammatical form and positioning for sentence parts separated by correlative conjunctions.**
   not only...but also...   **both...and...**
   either...or...   **neither...nor...**
                     whether...or...
   1. Although the bar was closed, she ordered not only a martini, but she also asked for two beers.
   ◆   Although the bar was closed, she ordered not only a martini but also two beers.

PRACTICE 6A: Revise the following sentences to improve the parallel structure.

1. Knowing the rules of grammar and to follow them makes a piece of writing more orderly and with more clarity.
2. Harry prefers writing business letters rather than to have a date.
3. Waldo either will attend NICC or he will enroll at UNI.
4. To issue a response would be magnifying the problem.
5. A work alert went out to Francis Flunk, Missy Work, and to Dorothy Dropped.
6. The fast pace of contemporary society threatens the development and growing of children's personalities.
7. Both the coach and those who assist her were awarded conference honors last season.
8. Since writing is controlled by purpose, the writer's purpose determines selection and how he organizes the content.

PRACTICE 6B: Add a smoother flow to the style of the sentences listed below by adding parallel structure after the double bars (//).

1. While walking in the woods today, I saw // three French hens, two turtle doves, and...
2. He // not only looks energetic but...
3. As we were leaving the airport, the weather forecast warned of // gale-force winds, pea-sized hail, and...
4. Madeline gave a lecture // about her trip to Ireland and ...
5. // To the non-sports enthusiast, golf on TV may seem boring, but...
6. The Dean of Students displayed // a stoic expression, a monotone voice, and ...
7. Her family members were // not only proud but...// by her success.
8. The class members were annoyed not so much // by the course requirements as ...
9. The manager insisted // that all work be handed in promptly and ...
10. Most employees come with // both a positive attitude...

MANGLED MEANING

Misplaced, Dangling, Squinting Modifiers

Misplaced Modifiers: place words, phrases, clauses as close as possible to the words they modify.

> **For Sale: Beautiful Yamaha piano by professor with attractive oak legs.** Who has the oak legs?

From newspaper article: **"Soviet leader Mikhail Gorbachev and President Reagan sign the historic arms control agreement banning intermediate range missiles in the East Room of the White House."** What area of the world will be protected from missile bombing?

> **From newspaper headline: "High School honors student charged with killing family members, friend"**
> Why is this student being honored for killing?

PRACTICE 6C: Reword the following examples to add clarity by eliminating misplaced modifiers.
1. Two college dorms were reported ransacked by the Peosta police.
2. In Iowa, a calf was born to a farmer with two heads.
3. The college's cafeteria serves beverages to students in little cans.
4. A new computer was donated to the Human Resources Department, which has caused a lot of trouble.
5. Her godfather Elmo gave little Marissa a new doll for Christmas called "Little Cuddles."
6. Working on her letter, the dog distracted Gladys.
7. The fawn was missed by the swerving semi which was standing in the middle of the highway.
8. Professor Wright bought a composition book for his library that costs $12.50.

Dangling Modifiers

A dangling modifier does not modify any word in its sentence. To correct dangling modifiers, add a word (person) that the phrase can sensibly modify, or change the phrase into a clause (contains a subject & verb).

Smoking a cigar, the bear stood on its hind legs.
Does the bear smoke cigars?

Following the scent, the lost skiers were located.
Are the skiers following the scent?

PRACTICE 6D: Revise the following sentences to clarify the dangling modifiers.

1. Lying on the hammock for three hours, the sun's rays grew hotter and hotter.
2. After pulling my three teeth, my gums felt sore.
3. At the age of four, my mother gave birth to my younger brother.
4. In preparing this letter, a detailed outline will be required.
5. Coming up the front walk, the mailbox was located near the front door.
6. After spending all night in the library, exhaustion overcame me.
7. At the age of ten, my family took a vacation to the Grand Titan Mountains.
8. While visiting with friends recently, the topic of employment came up.

Squinting Modifiers

Squinting modifiers are placed in such a way that they could modify two words. Move the modifier from the middle of the sentence to the beginning or end of the sentence to clarify meaning.

Waldo said on his way home he would stop to buy snacks.
Did Waldo say it on his way home, or will he stop on his way home?

Judith only has composition on Monday evenings.
Is Judith the only composition student; does she only have composition; or does the class meet only on Monday evenings?

PRACTICE 6E: Reword the following sentences for clarity by adjusting squinting modifiers.

1. I only told the police officer what I had seen.
2. I almost ate the whole pie.
3. Hilda said during the meeting the manager belched three times.

4. My daughter was advised frequently to submit her tax forms.
5. Jack was told the next day to register for next semester's classes.

PRACTICE 6F: Reword the following sentences for clarity by adjusting misplaced, dangling, or squinting modifiers.

1. The student was referred to the Writing Center with misplaced modifier problems.
2. Tom will make plans tomorrow to publish his writing.
3. At four-years-old, my mother took me to swimming lessons.
4. While dressing for work, the doorbell rang.
5. Zelmo was told often to eliminate squinting modifiers.
6. Kerry Wood soaked his arm he strained in ice.
7. Driving down the winding road, the duck and her ducklings halted traffic for five minutes.
8. Tom saw the swans swimming in the lake on the way to work.
9. Watching the evening news, Liz's pet hamster escaped from its cage.
10. Looking back through 45 years, many people who influenced my life come to mind.

CHAPTER 7

Conciseness / Cut the Deadwood

"Less is more." Good writers revise every sentence for conciseness until they are satisfied that every phrase cannot be rewritten more succinctly without sacrificing clarity. In their classic on writing, *The Elements of Style*, William Strunk, Jr., and E.B. White say, "Vigorous writing is concise. A sentence should contain no unnecessary words, a paragraph no unnecessary sentences, for the same reason that drawing should have no unnecessary lines and a machine no unnecessary parts. This requires not that writers make all their sentences short or that they avoid all detail and treat the subject only in outline, but that every word tells" (23). Usually reduction for conciseness occurs during the revision stage of the writing process. In his book *On Writing*, famous novelist Stephen King suggests the following formula for conciseness: "2nd draft =1st draft − 10%" (222). So, revise for conciseness to develop a tighter, more readable writing style.

Six Ways to Cut Deadwood

1. **Use strong, action-packed verbs.**
   Jim is a composition teacher at NICC. (7)
       Jim teaches composition at NICC. (5)
   Writers have to revise for conciseness. (6)
       Writers must revise for conciseness. (5)
   Good writers do the job of revising for conciseness. (9)
       Good writers revise for conciseness. (5)

2. **Cut <u>who,</u> <u>which,</u> <u>that</u> from your writing whenever possible.**
   Mark Twain, who is a famous American writer, wrote Tom Sawyer in 1876. (12)
       Mark Twain, a famous American writer, wrote Tom Sawyer in 1876. (10)

The letter that I gave you came from the Dean of Students. (12)

> I gave you the letter from the Dean of Students. (10)

3. **Avoid repetition of the same word or idea.**

In my opinion, I feel composition should be required of all college students. (13)

> Composition should be required of all college students. (8)

It is obvious that our college's basketball record could dip down into the lower half of the conference standings. (19)

> Obviously our college's basketball record could dip into the lower half of the conference standings. (15)

4. **Avoid wasted word groups like <u>I think</u>, <u>I feel</u>, <u>I believe</u>, <u>In my opinion</u>.**

I think that the Cardinals should win the pennant this season. (11)

> The Cardinals should win the pennant this season. (8)

5. **Eliminate unnecessary adverbs, especially <u>definitely</u>, <u>just</u>, <u>quite</u>, <u>really</u>, <u>very</u>.**

The insurance agent really enjoyed his new job. (8)

> The insurance agent loved his new job. (7)

The writer's creative work shows that he is very smart. (10)

> The writer's creative work shows his intelligence. (7)

6. **Combine sentences when the first word or reference of a second sentence repeats the last word of the previous sentence.**

For junior high, I went to Jefferson. Jefferson was a whole new experience for me. (15)

> I attended Jefferson Junior High, which became a whole new experience for me. (13)

All the boys in the neighborhood were jealous of my new racing bike. The bike went faster and jumped farther than any other bike around. (25)

> The boys in my neighborhood were jealous of my new racing bike, which went faster and jumped higher than any other bike around. (23)

That summer my parents moved to Buena Vista. That is where they had their first daughter. (16)

> That summer my parents moved to Buena Vista, where Mom had their first daughter. (14)

More Ways to cut Deadwood

1. **Write in active voice.**

   The composition students were assigned a research paper by the instructor. (11)

   > The composition instructor assigned his students a research paper. (9)

   A research paper will be written by the students in this course. (12)

   > Students in this course will write a research paper. (9)

2. **Reduce clauses to phrases and phrases to single words.**

   Because we found no one in the supervisor's office, we left a note. (13)

   > Finding no one in the supervisor's office, we left a note. (11)

   The employees decided that they would start their assignments early. (10)

   > The employees decided to start their assignments early. (8)

   The tennis players who came from California were scheduled for the third day of the competition. (16)

   > The tennis players from California were scheduled for day three of the competition. (13)

   Stephen King, who is a fine novelist, published another book this year. (12)

   > Stephen King, a fine novelist, published another book this year. (10)

   The seminars that were canceled will be rescheduled. (8)

   > Canceled seminars will be rescheduled. (5)

   Zelmo wrote all of his business letters in a conscientious way. (11)

   > Zelmo wrote his business letters conscientiously. (6)

3. **Eliminate dummy subjects—There is (are), Here is (are), It is (was).**

   There are seven ways I have found to reduce wordiness. (10)

   > I have found seven ways to reduce wordiness. (8)

   It is apparent that William Shakespeare was a brilliant writer. (10)

   > William Shakespeare wrote brilliantly. (4)

4. **Eliminate fillers like <u>The reason is … because</u> or <u>The thing that I am looking forward to is …</u>**

   The reason we are studying this concept is to eliminate wasted words in writing. (14)

We are studying this concept to eliminate wasted words in writing. (11)

The thing that I am looking forward to is attending a Celine Dione concert next year. (16)

I am looking forward to attending a Celine Dione concert next year. (12)

5.   **Remove –ing words whenever possible.**

The instructor was reading the class's essays for six hours. (10)

The instructor read the class's essays for six hours. (9))

PRACTICE 7A: Reduce wordiness in the following word groups taken from student essays.

1. due to the fact that	8. be in agreement with	15. control over
2. at this point in time	9. few in number	16. sinks down
3. exact same spot	10. huddled together	17. descend down
4. raised up	11. merge together	18. calmed myself down
5. finished up	12. passes by	19. green in color
6. gather up	13. replied back	20. It is obvious that
7. ended up	14. return back	21. smile on his face

PRACTICE 7B: Reduce the wordiness in the following examples.

1. We went and checked in.
2. I proceeded to start the car.
3. I very much feared…
4. I raced off in a sprint.
5. I completely told her everything.
6. I wondered to myself…
7. They pretty much became resentful of each other.
8. My brother replied by saying…
9. Three and four days passed us by.
10. It unites everyone together.
11. The inside of my truck is definitely not the neatest.
12. Cindy's father decided to resign. The resignation was a shock to everyone.
13. I also have some very strange luck.
14. I definitely ran down the stairs faster than I have ever moved in my entire life.
15. I quickly lost any momentary compassion I possessed toward the snake.
16. I didn't get much sleep that night.

17. We lined up in the cafeteria so that everyone could tell us congratulations.

18. There are some people in America who don't mind that illegal immigrants enter this country.

19. I was taught at a very young age to respect guns.

20. The reason for returning to school is because I want to make a better life for my family and me.

PRACTICE 7C: Reduce the wordiness in the following sentences.

1. It is evident that some employees decided to hand in their business correspondence early in order that they might receive added vacation days. (23)

2. After the agent had looked everywhere for a research article on Medicare, he finally copied a section of information that he found in his insurance manual. (26)

3. The vacation that we took to Seattle last year would have been perfect if it had not been for all the rain that fell each day we were there. (29)

4. Since we were sitting in seats right behind home plate in Wrigley Field, we were able to analyze and judge the accuracy of the home plate umpire's calls. (28)

5. The most common complaint that is made by employees at this company is that all supervisors choose the same day on which to evaluate their personnel. (26)

CHAPTER 8

Say What You Mean. Mean What You Say!

"Not only does specific language serve as clarification and evidence, but it also adds interest. It can spice up a passage that might otherwise be bland" (37).
– Robert Miles

Be Specific!

In your writing, try to be as exact and specific as possible to give readers the clearest picture of the meaning you intend. Note the following examples:

Vague: The disgruntled composition teacher entered the classroom a little late.

Specific: Professor Waldo Wright ripped open the door to his 8 AM English Composition I classroom at 8:12 and threw his attaché case on the desk.

Vague: The lady bought lots of items at the mall for which she paid too much.

Specific: Sarah Spends left Kennedy Mall with three dresses, two hats, two pairs of slacks, and five pairs of earrings for which she paid $812.

PRACTICE 8A: Substitute specific wording for the following:

1. person
2. city
3. musical group
4. college
5. food
6. athlete
7. vehicle
8. smell
9. restaurant
10. song
11. cap
12. supervisor

PRACTICE 8B: Substitute specific action words for the following:

1. eat	4. drink	7. talk	10. look
2. touch	5. run	8. hit	11. catch
3. complain	6. sing	9. start	12. ask

PRACTICE 8C: Rewrite the following sentences to make them specific and exact.

1. The young man read a magazine until very late yesterday evening.
2. The person placed his tools in the truck.
3. We talked about a touchy issue.
4. We went to the city, ate at a restaurant, and then attended a concert.
5. My pet ran away this morning, and a citizen on the other end of town found her in a park near his business.
6. The student attends college, works in a restaurant, and plays an instrument in a band.
7. A college instructor has written a business writing book, according to the weekly newspaper.
8. The kid got into the car quickly and drove from the scene rapidly.

When writing paragraphs, use specific, concrete nouns early in each paragraph as antecedents for later pronoun references. Avoid vague nouns (a person, people) and pronouns (one, you, he, she, it, they). Also in your paragraphs, maintain consistency of verb tenses (present-past), person (first-third), and number (singular-plural).

Correct Word Usage

The difference between the right word and the almost-right word is the difference between lightning and a lightning-bug" (162). – Mark Twain

The following word usage situations frequently arise in writing, but your computer may not detect or offer the correct usage. Fill in the spaces with the correct usage.

1. **accept** – verb "to receive";   **except** – preposition "excluding"
   We _____ your invitation.
   If you _____ his first semester's grades, he has accumulated
       a good grade point.
   My grades appear satisfactory in every course _____ physics.

2. **affect** – verb "to influence, to   **effect** – noun "result"
   cause";   ("tip" – action = **verb** = **affect**)
   How did the defeat _____ the team?
   Everyone felt the _____ of the strike.

3. **all right** & **a lot** - always spelled as two words, not "alright, alot."

4. **alumna**=singular female; **alumnae**=plural females;
   alumnus=singular male; **alumni**=plural males or both genders.
   My wife Kay is an _____ of Clarke College.
   Her husband Jim is an _____ of Loras College.
   Mark and Mary are _____ of the University of
       Dubuque.

5. **amount** – use with a singular   **number** – use with a plural word.
   word;
   She always carried a small _____ of money.
   The Bears' line displays a tremendous _____ of power.
   A _____ of fumbles occurred during the second quarter.
   He held a _____ of coins in his hand.

6. **although** – subordinating   **however** – adverb; meaning "on the
   conjunction; introduces a   other hand" or "by contrast."
   dependent clause.
   _____ it was 10 degrees below zero, I didn't feel a
       thing.
   It was 10 degrees below zero; _____, I didn't feel a
       thing.

7. **bad** – adjective (modifies   **badly** - adverb (modifies verb,
   noun or pronoun);   adjective, adverb)
   The Cubs play _____.
   The stockyards smell _____.

8. **beside** – "by the side of"   **besides** – adv. "in addition to" or
   someone or something   prep. "except"

Along came a spider and sat down _____ her.
He owned nothing _____ his good name.
He received a medal and five dollars _____ .

9. **between** – use with two;   **among** – use with more than two.
   The ball was passed _____ Phil and you.
   We earned two dollars _____ the five of us.

10. **borrow** – "to get with the   **lend** – "to give someone something
    intention of returning"   you expect to get back"

    I _____ some money from my father.
    Lisa didn't want to _____ me any of her clothes.

11. **bring**–denotes motion   **take**—denotes motion away from
    toward a place;   a place
    _____ my business letter here.
    _____ my business letter there.

12. **can**–expresses ability;   **may**–expresses permission or
                                       possibility
    _____ I accompany you to the dance?
    _____ you type 3,000 words per minute?

13. **could of, should of, would of** – of is not a verb.
    correct = **could have, should have, would have**

    The composition instructor should of given us more work.
    The compositon instructor should _____ given us more work.

14. **due to** or **due to the fact that** - use since, because, or because of,
    unless **due** functions as predicate adjective.
    Nonstandard: Due to the fact that we have so much rain, the
    game is cancelled.
    Correct: Because we have so much rain, the game is cancelled.

15. **fewer** – use with a plural   **less** – use with a singular word.
    word;
    I encounter _____ health problems than I did 10 years ago.
    I save _____ money than I did 10 years ago.

16. **good** – adjective, modifies a   **well** – adverb – "perform an action
    noun;   capably" or adjective – "in good
                                           health," "satisfactory"

    The Cardinals played _____ against the Cubs.
    Violet sang _____ in the concert.
    Herman does not feel _____ after eating four pizzas.
    Otto appears to be in _____ health.
    Ellen looks _____ in that new, blue dress.
    His clothes never fit him _____.

17. **imply** – "to suggest   **infer** – "to interpret, to conclude"
    something";   from.
    A writer or speaker _____ to a reader or listener.
    A reader or listener _____ from a writer or speaker.

18. **in** – "located within";   **into** – "from the outside into"
    We were all gathered _____ my grandparents' living room.
    Joe just walked _____ my office.

19. **irregardless** – drop **IR** – should be <u>regardless</u>.
    _____ of the score, our team won.

20. **it's** – "it is";   **its** – possessive
    Dubuque proudly boasts of _____ hills.
    _____ not too late.
    _____ a long way to Tipperary.
    The dog chewed on _____ bone.

21. **lay** – "put or place" (lay,   **lie** –"rest or recline" (lie, lying, lay,
    laying, laid, laid);   lain)
    Last night Homer _____ in his bed all night.
    Waldo _____ his gun on the table.
    _____ the dish on the counter.
    I plan to _____ in the sun this afternoon.

22. **leave** – "to go away from";   **let** – "to allow or permit"
    I am _____ my past life behind.
    I will _____ him have my answer soon.
    We will _____ if you _____ us.

23. **like** – preposition,   **as** or **as if** – subordinating
    introduces a phrase;   conjunction–introduces a clause.
    She looks _____ a queen.
    She does _____ she wishes.

24. **principal**—(noun or adjective) noun: person in a high position or
    important role; adjective: means "chief" or "most important." Also,
    a sum of money lent or borrowed.
    principle—(only a noun) guiding rule or fundamental truth.
    Kay provides the _____ income in our family.
    The _____ of your school acts like your "pal."
    It opposed his _____ to give easy grades.
    I pay the _____ on my homeowner's loan.

25. **rise** – "to go up" (rise, rose,   **raise**–"to force something up" (raise,
    risen);   raised, raised)
    The sun is _____ in the sky.
    The farmer _____ two chickens and two daughters.

26. **set** – "to put or place";   **sit** – "to seat yourself"
    Please _____ down.
    Please _____ your glass down.

27. **than** – used in comparisons;   **then** – adverb of time
    Hilda seems stronger _____ Waldo.
    She ate breakfast and _____ brushed her teeth.
    _____ the waiter handed us the bill.
    Our house costs more _____ theirs.

28. **double negative** – **can't hardly, can't scarcely** (hardly and scarcely
    are negatives when combined with <u>not</u>), **can't help but; no,
    nothing, none** combined with **not**.
    Examples of Nonstandard Usage:
    I can't hardly tell the difference between this year's cars and last
        year's.
    There wasn't scarcely enough food for everyone.
    Haven't you no ticket?
    I can't help but admire his courage.
    She hasn't nothing to do.
    He didn't give me none.

PRACTICE 8D: Word Usage   Correct word usage errors in the following sentences. Some may be correct.

1. They have met less students from UNI than from NICC.
2. How will the new policies effect the employees?
3. Besides my instructors, my friends have been pushing me to study.
4. Both of the women giving speeches are alumnae of NICC.
5. The cash prizes were divided between the six winners.
6. Researchers are studying the effects of the new drug.
7. I could of written a better letter if I had edited more closely.
8. I hope you will take your children when you come to Florida this summer.
9. As you grow older, you will find less chances to change jobs.
10. She excepted our congratulations with deep appreciation.
11. The amount of pizzas Zelmo can eat astounds me.
12. I see growing awareness of good writing among the employees.
13. With three jobs to choose from, Waldo couldn't decide which one to accept.
14. The composition instructor complained about the amount of papers not turned in.
15. In his novels, Hemingway implies that war unjustly costs many innocent lives.
16. My boss is borrowing me $5,000.
17. I asked my friends to leave me go with them to the gym.
18. His comments inferred that he did not agree with the new policy.
19. Should writers be held responsible for what readers infer from their works?
20. If he had behaved like he should, he wouldn't be steeped in trouble now.
21. The composition instructor left us use the writing lab after class.
22. Bring a computer with you when you fly to North Buenie.
23. Zelmo had made a large amount of friends.
24. The response shows how much the readers were effected by the business letter.
25. I can't hardly read your business writing.

PRACTICE 8E: Word Usage

1. You might of found it hard to finish your letter for Tuesday.
2. Leave me give you some good writing tips.

3. Beside his interest in poetry, Waldo also enjoys business letter writing.
4. The volcano has been acting like it might erupt.
5. The instructor asked the class less questions than he had prepared.
6. What effect will the new assignment have on the company?
7. I can't find nothing else to worry about.
8. Paula seldom edits as good as she should.
9. I'll bring my portfolio to Herman's room when I go.
10. Due to the storm, writing classes were cancelled last Friday.
11. Someone had ought to bring snacks to the writing sessions.
12. I must have laid in bed for an hour after the alarm sounded.
13. Because of his cold, Donald did not feel good yesterday.
14. A heavy mist laid in the valley.
15. The temperature in this room is raising.
16. The documents laying on my desk need my signature.
17. I plan to lay in bed all day Saturday.
18. Marian did good on her business writing exam.
19. You might have found less friends than he.

CHAPTER 9

Action Verbs, Active Voice, Avoiding Shifts

*"Colorful, vibrant verbs produce persuasive,
dynamic, specific writing. They energize and
uplift your writing. A strong verb evokes imagery
and movement. In contrast, a weak verb seems
vague or lethargic" (109).* – Elizabeth Danziger

DEVELOPING A STRONG STYLE THROUGH ACTION VERBS

Strong, action-packed verbs invigorate, energize, and tighten writing style. Columnist Joan Beck calls verbs the vibrant heart of the sentence and says, "Verbs pump action into the message. They energize static nouns into motion and jab predicates into shape. Verbs tease, purr, shout, intrigue, hook, motivate" (Scott 57).

A writing style demonstrating strong, lively verbs will serve a number of purposes. Writing becomes more precise, exciting, and forceful. By allowing the writer to omit unnecessary words, verb strength also helps condense phrases and sentences, for as Robert Southey says, "Words are like sunbeams – the more they are condensed, the deeper they burn" (Perrine). In addition, writers broaden their vocabularies, which fosters a more interesting, specific style. Verb strength also forces writers beyond simple sentence structures into a variety of patterns, such as dependent clauses, phrases, and appositives.

When revising and editing, writers should identify weak, overused verbs which tend to deaden style and increase wordiness. Then they should substitute specific, action-packed verbs for the following at every opportunity:

- **DO**: do, doing, does, did, done
  Walter does his writing at the kitchen table can be rewritten **Walter writes at the kitchen table.**

- **HAVE**: have, having, has, had
  The rotten egg has a putrid smell can be rewritten
  The rotten egg smells putrid.

- **BE**: am, is, are, was, were, be, being, been
  There are many examples to show that this team is great can be rewritten
  Many examples show the greatness of this team.

Note that forms of <u>do</u> (do, does, did, done), <u>have</u> (have, has, had), and <u>be</u> (am, is, are, was, were, be, been) might be used as helping verbs to form various tenses. The sentence, *"I have four rabbits"* uses a weak verb <u>have</u> as the main verb while **"I have revised my writing for verb strength"** uses the helping verb <u>have</u> with the main verb <u>revised</u>. Writers may use forms of <u>do</u>, <u>have</u>, and <u>be</u> as helping (auxiliary) verbs but should try to avoid them as main (primary) verbs.

As writers use stronger, more specific verbs, they develop sentence structure variety which provides a livelier style. For example, *"Jay Gatsby is the protagonist of a novel in which he is deceitful and cunning in order to win back his love, Daisy Buchanan"* can be revised by eliminating the weak verb <u>is</u> and by using an appositive: **"Jay Gatsby, the novel's cunning protagonist, uses deception to win back his first love, Daisy Buchanan."** This sentence could also be written using a dependent clause: **"When Jay Gatsby, the novel's protagonist, uses deception, he wins back his first love, Daisy Buchanan."**

As writers eliminate weak verbs, they sometimes replace the <u>be</u> forms with other unconvincing verb phrases. This practice also leads to wordiness and a sense of uncertainty in writing. Therefore, avoid replacing <u>be</u> forms with **seems, appears to be, exists as,** or **proves to be** or replacing <u>have/has</u> with **possesses**. These verbs only replace verb shallowness, enhance wordiness, and cause writing style to feel forced. For example, *"It seems to be snowing in Florida"* can be reduced to **"It is snowing in Florida."** *"Fred often possesses a smiling face"* can be revised to read **"Fred smiles often."**

Sentences beginning with *"There is (was), There are (were)"* or *"It is (was)"* will also force writers into using weak verbs. *"There are millions of Americans who love baseball"* can be revised to **"Millions of Americans love baseball."** *"It is necessary for writers to analyze their styles for vigorous verbs"* can be revised to **"Writers should analyze their styles for vigorous verbs."** In addition to adding a more forceful, energetic tone, eliminating *"There is (are)"* and *"It is (was)"* at the beginning of sentences helps develop a tighter, more economic writing style.

Writers can also enhance their verb strength by avoiding nominalization – adding suffixes such as –ion to verbs to form nouns. Whenever possible, rewrite sentences by transferring an –ion ending noun into a verb. *"It is the company's intention to give the workers a raise,"* for example, uses the noun <u>intention</u> which becomes the verb <u>intends</u> in the following revision: **"This company intends to give the workers a raise."** The following example demonstrates the same idea. *"The administration made the decision to drop the athletic program"* might be revised to **"The administration decided to drop the athletic program."** Notice how the noun <u>decision</u> (ending in –ion) can form a more forceful verb <u>decided</u>. Besides <u>–ion</u>, "some other noun endings smother verbs: <u>-ance</u>, <u>-ment</u>, <u>-ancy</u>, <u>-ant</u>, <u>-ent</u>, <u>-able</u>" (Scott 57). Nouns ending in these suffixes can easily be converted to verbs like:

He has dominance over	—	he dominates
They are in agreement	—	they agree
They are in violation of	—	they violate
Her contention is	—	she contends that.

Initially writers may find revising sentences for verb strength painful and time-consuming since they have relied on the same weak verbs for most of their writing lives. However, after a bit of practice, writers find revising with vigorous verbs both challenging and rewarding. In addition, a lively, economic writing style reinforces the value of this revision strategy.

PRACTICE 9A: WEAK VERBS vs. HELPING VERBS.　Write all helping verbs in the left column and the main verbs in the right column. Remember, a main verb may be preceded by none, one, two, or three helping verbs. Also, main verbs may be separated from their helping verbs by adverbs, like <u>not</u>.

	Helping Verbs	Main Verbs

1. Wilmer had not finished his document yet.
2. He must have been planning to complete it over the weekend.
3. He should have asked the supervisor for help.
4. But he felt foolish,
5. so he never approached the supervisor.
6. Do you believe Wilmer's apprehension?
7. Our supervisor would surely have understood.
8. He would probably even have extended the deadline for Wilmer.
9. Or would this supervisor go that far?
10. We will never know.

PRACTICE 9B: STYLE-VERB STRENGTH. Tighten and liven style by revising the following sentences to eliminate weak verbs.

1. My name is Robin Goodfellow. I was born on January 12, 1984, at Story County Hospital.
2. I have a few worries about my career choice, but anything that is worthwhile will not be an easy task.
3. After I was laid off, I knew I was going to go back to school. This was a hard decision for me because I have been out of school for over 30 years and because I have children who are now in college.
4. My parents' names are Herman and Hilda. They gave each of my brothers names that start with "H."
5. My sister is eleven, and she is in fourth grade at Romper Room Elementary School.
6. I am currently in the business world. It is a big change from college life.

7. There were a lot of open fields and wild timber to explore.
8. When I was a little girl, I read a book called *Grimm's Fairy Tales*.
9. My parents are Mickey and Minnie Mouse. Until recently, they have lived in Disneyland.
10. I could be a writer with all the adventures I've had.

PRACTICE 9C: STYLE-VERB STRENGTH.   Tighten and liven style by revising the following paragraphs to eliminate weak verbs. Then count the number of words in your revised paragraphs.

I.   I have many memories from the past 18 years. There are plenty of years left to make more, but some of the greatest ones are in the past. I have a lot of accomplishments, but still have more to come. I am anxious for the new challenges of college life. Over the past years, when a problem would arise, there were familiar people to help me. Now it's a whole new world. (73 words)

II.   My high school was very small. It had about 110 kids in all four grades. My graduating class was about as big as my immediate family. However, even though it was small, it taught me the ropes of what future schooling would be like. Not only did I learn through the classes, but also through sports, as well. Basketball and baseball were the only two sports the school had to offer, and I was in love with both of them. (80 words)

VOICE: ACTIVE & PASSIVE

Verbs in the passive voice are dressed for a funeral; they have about them a tone of stiff formality which, perhaps, accounts for their irresistibility to those who…speak in a cemetery voice" (44).– Irving Younger

Generally, business writers prefer active voice over passive voice because active voice is more vigorous, emphatic, forceful, direct, and concise. The passive voice requires two more words than the active voice. In an active voice sentence, the subject does the action; in the passive voice, something is done to the subject. The passive voice can be recognized by TO BE form helping verbs plus a past participle. In addition, most passive sentences end in a by _____ prepositional phrase. Note the difference in voice in the following examples:

PASSIVE: The business letter was written by Sharon.
ACTIVE: Sharon wrote the business letter.

Occasionally, the passive voice may be favored 1) when the doer of the action is unknown, 2) to place the focus on the receiver of the action.

Examples: 1) My computer was stolen last night.
2) An error in judgment has been made by the registrar in the calculations of the student's grades.

Remember:

Use active voice whenever possible for a stronger, more concise writing style.

Using three steps, writers can easily change passive voice verbs into active voice.

1. **Flip the sentence.** Make the object of the preposition _by_ the subject of the sentence. The passive voice subject then becomes the object of the sentence.
2. **Eliminate TO BE verb forms (am, is, are, was, were, be, been)** used as helping verbs.
3. **Keep helping verbs has-have, had, will,** which form the perfect and future tenses. This preserves tense consistency.

Examples:

PASSIVE: The gerbils have been fed by my roommate.
(present perfect tense)
ACTIVE: My roommate has fed the gerbils.

PASSIVE: A new computer was bought by my writing partner.
(past tense)
ACTIVE: My writing partner bought a new computer.

PASSIVE: A Writing Center conference is needed by Clarence.
(present tense)
ACTIVE: Clarence needs a Writing Center conference.

Note: The helping verbs am, is, are signal present tense.

*"If you are blessed with confidence, whether it be
innate or earned as a result of knowing you've
mastered your subject, you'll almost instinctively
employ the active voice, since it will be natural
for you to assert what you know, and to assert it
in bold terms. If, however, you are fundamentally
insecure about your thesis, you'll almost instinctively
turn to the passive voice as a refuge" (64).* –John R. Trimble

PRACTICE 9D: Revise the following sentences by changing passive voice verbs to active voice verbs.

1. The expectations explained in the course syllabus must be met by all composition students.
2. Business letters have been processed by each employee, and they will be shared at the next staff meeting.
3. Ankle-supported basketball shoes were used by many college basketball players over the years.
4. Flu shots had been given to the majority of the first year class by the college's medical staff.
5. Active voice sentences are preferred over passive voice sentences by most good writers.

PRACTICE 9E: Revise the following passage by changing passive voice sentences to active voice.

Robert Frost

Born in San Francisco in 1874, poet Robert Frost was raised by his mother in New England after his father died. Dartmouth and Harvard were both attended by Frost, but he did not graduate from college. Farming and rural New England life were loved by Frost, and these subjects were addressed prominently in his poetry. Frost was married to Elinor White, and he, along with his wife and children, moved to England in 1912 to farm and write. In 1913, Frost's first book, *A Boy's Will*, was published by Englishman David Nutt. Two years later the Frost family returned to New England, and for the rest of his life, Frost was heralded as a major American poet. The Pulitzer Prize was awarded to Frost four times. In 1961, Frost was invited by President John F. Kennedy to read the poem "The Gift Outright" at the Presidential Inauguration. Robert Frost died in 1963 in Boston, but his poetry lives prominently in American literature.

UNNECESSARY SHIFTS IN TENSE, VOICE, PERSON

        past tense   *present tense*

TENSE: I **wrote** four pages of my essay when my computer **starts** to malfunction.

        1ˢᵗ person   *2ⁿᵈ person*

PERSON: Anyone like **me** would feel frustrated after **you** wrote four

        1ˢᵗ person   *2ⁿᵈ person*

pages of **my** persuasive essay, and then **your** computer started to malfunction.

        active voice

VOICE: I **planned** to register for next semester's classes, but most of the

        passive   *voice*

sections **had** already **been filled** by sophomores.

    The three examples above illustrate unnecessary shifts in tense, person, and voice. Writers must try to retain consistency in these three areas so they do not confuse or annoy their readers. Consistency in tense, person, and voice requires conscientious revising and editing.

TENSE: Perhaps the most annoying shift to a reader involves tense (present, past, future) because the verb carries the main action and the sense of time. Shifting tenses illogically within a sentence or group of sentences can mislead or contradict the intended meaning of a passage. Obviously, verb tenses will need to change when they indicate obvious time changes.

PERSON: The English conjugation system uses three persons: first person (I, me, we, us) refers to the writer or speaker; second person (you) refers to the reader or listener; and third person (he, she, it, they) refers to people being written or spoken about. Most shifts occur when writers jump from first or third person into second person.

VOICE: Revise/edit carefully to avoid unnecessary shifts from active to passive voice. In the active voice, the subject of the verb acts. In the passive voice, the subject of the verb is acted upon. Many times a shift in voice causes a shift in subject matter. If you begin a sentence in the active voice, do not shift to passive voice, and vice versa.

PRACTICE 9F: Revise the following sentences to adjust inconsistencies in tense, person, or voice.

1. The President of the College reads a statement to the student body but refused to respond to any questions.
2. If first year college students expect to earn good grades, you need to organize your time and study habits consistently.
3. Students should not expect to rely on their parents for all their financial support because you need to support yourself as an adult.
4. When you feel the flu coming on, employees should rest and drink plenty of fluids.
5. When we go to Florida for spring break, you visited the beach for sun and fun.
6. The wide receiver caught the pass and weaves his way through three defenders toward the end zone.
7. We leave for work at 11 o'clock, and a sub-sandwich was eaten on the way.
8. If a person likes to see thrilling drama, you should watch Mel Gibson's portrayal of Hamlet.
9. The supervisor reads the first employee's letter, and the third letter is read forty-five minutes later.
10. The manager read the report, and then the response was written.

PRACTICE 9G: Rewrite the following passage to provide consistency in tense, person, and voice.

Henry David Thoreau lived from 1817 to 1862 around Concord, Massachusetts. Thoreau was provided a Harvard education by his father, who earned a living as a pencil maker. For two years, he was housed by Ralph Waldo Emerson, his long-time friend. At age 28, a small cabin was built on the shore of Walden Pond near Concord. Thoreau lives there for two years, and his famous book *Walden* is published in 1854. Although the natural charms of the woods are described in the book, Thoreau's comments on simple living and deep thinking were recognized as a major contribution to 19th century American thinking. Although Thoreau does not urge you to imitate his example of solitary living, it was followed by many who had read *Walden*.

# CHAPTER 10

"Let's Come to Agreement"

Subject-Verb Agreement

1. The subject and verb of a sentence must agree in number (singular or plural) and gender.

Singular:	The composition student writes the essays.
Plural:	The composition students write the essays.

Singular:	She goes to work at 8 a.m.
Plural:	They go to work at 8 a.m.

Singular:	The office closes at 5 p.m.
Plural:	The offices close at 5 p.m.

Note: A verb in the third person singular, present tense, ends in −s and requires a singular subject. The ending −s on a subject, however, usually signals plural and requires a plural verb, not ending in −s. Note the following exceptions, however:

Mumps is a bad disease.
Economics has given me lots of trouble.
Mathematics is much harder than English.
My boss treats me fairly.
Physics has to be taught well.
The waitress was hired for the lunch rush.

2. A company or corporation, even consisting of many names, is considered a single body requiring a singular verb.

Cottingham and Butler is a privately owned insurance firm founded in 1887.

Fuerste, Carew, Coyle, Juergens, & Sudmeier is a law firm in Dubuque.

Honkamp Krueger & Co., P.C. is a large company featuring certified public accountants and business consultants.

3. **A collective noun, referring to a group, uses a singular verb.**

The writing committee is meeting today.

The basketball team has been practicing for two weeks.

The news about the economy is shocking.

The Peosta City Council meets on Mondays.

4. **The subject of a sentence cannot be located in a prepositional phrase.**

The performance (of the secretaries) was excellent.

The decision (of the personnel managers) is final.

The supervisor (as well as the managers) was upset about the report.

The instructor (together with the students) does his best.

The Dean of Students (along with six professors) is flying to Chicago.

5. **Compound Subjects:**

If the compound subject parts are joined by **and**, make the verb **plural**.

If the compound subject parts are joined by **or** or **nor**, make the verb agree with the nearer(est) subject to the verb.

A new computer **and** printer were placed in every office.

Tom, Dick, **and** Harry want to participate in the writing seminar.

Either a new computer **or** a new printer was placed in every office.

Either Dick **or** Harry wants to participate in the seminar.

6. **Indefinite Pronouns:**

Singular: **each, either, neither, one, every, anyone, everyone, someone, anybody, everybody, somebody**

Everybody who can is encouraged to attend the writing seminar.

Everyone has his or her own ideas about social security.

Each of the students is given a course syllabus.

Neither of the computers works very well.

Plural: **several, few, both, many**

Several of the participants are late.

Few of my friends have taken their spring vacations.

Many are called; few are chosen.

Singular or Plural depending on the meaning of the sentence: **all, any, none, some, most, half, part**

All of the computer looks clean.

All of the computers look clean.

Most of the essay was lost.

Most of the essays were lost.

7. **Inversion: When a sentence begins with _Here_, _There_, _Where_, _Which_, or _What_, the subject will follow the verb.**

There are many writing guidelines to follow.

There is a vacant seat in the 10:30 a.m. composition class.

Here are the supplies the manager ordered.

Where are the surveys and reports?

What are our options in this matter?

8. **Book titles (_The Three Musketeers_), courses (economics), diseases (measles), or other words singular in meaning require a singular verb. Quantities such as miles, dollars, or years require a singular verb when the amount is considered a collective unit.**

Two Gentlemen of Verona was chosen as the next school production.

Physics is a tough class for Wanda.

The mumps usually lasts three days.

The Tenants by Bernard Malamud is an interesting novel.

Two hundred pounds is too heavy for a jockey.

Ten miles to the gallon was all I could get.

Eighty-one to nothing was the final score.

9. **The number of** requires **a singular** verb; **a number of** requires **a plural** verb.

The number of employees in the writing seminar is surprising.

A number of insurance agents have signed up for the writing seminar.

10. For graduates or former students of a school or college: **alumna** = singular female, **alumnae** = plural females; **alumnus** = singular male, **alumni** = plural males or both genders.

My wife Kay is an alumna of Clarke College.

My husband Jim is an alumnus of Loras College.

Mark and Mary are alumni of the University of Dubuque.

PRACTICE 10A: Choose the verb that agrees with the subject.

1. Mathematics (is, are) difficult for many people.
2. The boss (rides, ride) his bike to work each day.
3. The participants (is, are) ready to begin the seminar.
4. The Weber Paper Company (was, were) to call back by three o'clock today.
5. The construction of the new offices (was, were) begun last year.
6. Cottingham and Butler (is, are) an insurance firm located in downtown Dubuque.
7. Measles (is, are) a contagious disease.
8. The printer, in addition to the two computers, (needs, need) to be repaired.
9. *Snow White and the Seven Dwarfs* (is, are) a Disney film.
10. There (is, are) six participants sleeping throughout this seminar.
11. The writing in these seminars (is, are) improving rapidly.
12. Each of the administrative assistants (types, type) 120 words per hour.
13. Waldo, Ralph, and Fritz (has, have) started a new consulting business.
14. Either the supervisor or the employees (is, are) misinformed about the policy.
15. Eighty-five dollars (is, are) too much to pay for a composition book.
16. Here (is, are) six copies of the business document.
17. Which (is, are) your favorite type of writing assignments.
18. Neither Monday nor Tuesday (seems, seem) to fit into our schedules.
19. The number of horses in the parade (is, are) staggering.
20. Every one of my letters (is, are) too long.
21. The alumni (has, have) been contributing generously.
22. The choir of professors (sings, sing) at each Christmas party.
23. Some of the phones (needs, need) to be replaced.
24. One of the accountants (flies, fly) to Las Vegas each Thursday.

PRACTICE 10B: Edit the following sentences for subject-verb agreement.

1. Neither of the computer operators have transferred the data correctly.
2. The members of our staff is on the alert throughout the weekend.
3. Somebody in our offices is assigned to refill the printers.

4. Where's the clients you described?
5. A few of the maintenance staff stay behind to clean up the offices.
6. Business 212 were a tough course for any writing major.
7. Here's three options you can choose from.
8. One of the night watchmen were injured during the office Christmas party.
9. Neither her colleagues nor Lila is going to work overtime on Thursday.
10. The CEO's responses to our letter changes our strategy.
11. A police officer or an official from the parking commission are planning to address the students about improper parking.
12. Do either of the positions being advertised require special skills?
13. Several of the employees and management were given the day off.
14. Somebody with lots of brains lock the door from the outside.
15. Either Henry or the two secretaries is getting lunch for the CEO.

PRACTICE 10C: Write sentences demonstrating correct subject-verb agreement for the following formulas:

1. Write a sentence in the present tense with a singular subject.

2. Write a sentence in the present tense with a plural verb.

3. Write a sentence in the present tense whose subject and verb are separated by a prepositional phrase.

4. Write a sentence in the present tense using a singular indefinite pronoun as subject.

5. Write a sentence in the present tense using a plural indefinite pronoun as subject.

6. Write a sentence in the present tense with a compound subject joined by **and**.

7. Write a sentence in the present tense with a compound subject joined by **or**.

8. Write a sentence in the present tense with compound subjects joined by **either…or.**

9. Write a sentence in the present tense with a compound subject joined by **neither…nor.**

10. Write a sentence in the present tense beginning with the word **There, Here, Where, Which,** or **What.**

Pronoun-Antecedent Agreement

1. A pronoun and its antecedent must agree in number (singular and plural) and gender.

> The writer should clean off **her** desk. (singular)
> The writers should clean off **their** desks. (plural)
> Cottingham and Butler sent **its** client the proposal. (singular)

2. Use a plural pronoun to refer to a compound antecedent joined by <u>and</u>.

> Martha **and** her friend bought **their** plane tickets to Cancun.

3. When a compound antecedent is joined by <u>or</u> or <u>nor</u>, the pronoun agrees with the word closer(est) to the pronoun.

> Neither Miss Morton **nor** her department members have written **their** letters well.
> Either her department members **or** Miss Morton will write **her** essay again.

4. Indefinite Pronouns:

> a) Singular: **each, either, neither, one, every, anyone, everyone, someone, anybody, everybody, somebody**
> > **Every** student is working at **his or her** desk.
> > **Each** of the students turned in **his or her** essay.
> ****Note: Use a plural antecedent to add smoother sentence flow.**
> > All **employees** are working at **their** desks.
> > All **employees** submitted **their** proposals.
> b) Plural: **several, few, both, many**
> > **Both** of the accountants brought **their** own lunches.
> > **Few** of the complaints have reached **their** targets.

c) Singular or Plural depending on the meaning of the sentence:
all, any, none, some, most, half, part
All of the equipment was returned to **its** place.
All of the accountants like **their** new computers.
Half of the printers remained in **their** boxes.

PRACTICE 10D: Select the correct pronoun to agree with its antecedent.
1. All of the secretaries wish (she, they) could type as fast as Hilda.
2. The receptionist is good at (her, their) jobs.
3. Neither Frank nor Homer received (his, their) Christmas bonus.
4. Either the boss or the employees will take (his, their) vacations early.
5. All students looked happy when (he or she, they) picked up their grades.
6. Some of the letters need (its, their) envelopes retyped.
7. Either the ledger or the account book lost (its, their) cover.
8. Employees should monitor (his, their) own work.
9. The No-Doz Company likes (its, their) employees to stay awake.
10. Both the professors and the instructors earned (his or her, their) raises.

PRACTICE 10E: Edit the following sentences for pronoun-antecedent agreement.
1. Every writer should recognize their own special talents.
2. None of the letters were in its original folder.
3. All writers should revise their own letters for clarity.
4. Does anyone want their job to be interesting?
5. Either the accountant or the bookkeepers left his calculator in the lobby.
6. Few employees can give his or her explanation of the deficit.
7. Everyone created their own expectations.
8. Neither the debit nor the credit was posted in their proper column.
9. None of the appreciation was relayed to its recipient.
10. All employees were told to turn in his or her parking permits at the gate.

PRACTICE 10F: Complete the following using a pronoun to refer
to the subject provided.

1. Everyone in the class

2. All of the employees

3. Neither the instructor nor the students

4. Each of the receptionists

5. Few of the supervisors

6. Every participant in the seminar

7. Both of the auditors

8. Either the custodian or the night watchman

CHAPTER 11

Adjective-Adverb & Pronoun Usage
"Yous guys ain't done good!"

USING MODIFIERS CORRECTLY

	Modify:	Answer the questions:	
ADJECTIVES	nouns pronouns	what kind? which one?	how much? how many?
ADVERBS	verbs adjectives adverbs	how? where? when?	how much? how often?

ADJECTIVE	**ADVERB**
The **efficient** student	The student works **efficiently**.
The **new** computer	The computer **never** works **well**.
My boss is **honest**.	Her boss seems **completely** honest.

Points of Emphasis:

1. Most, not all, adverbs end in **–ly**. Note: adverbs such as **almost, much, never, not, often, quite, seldom, there, too, very** do not end in **–ly**.

Mary **often** speaks **cheerfully** in the morning.

2. Adjectives are often used after linking verbs (predicate adjectives). The most common **linking verbs** are: **act, appear, be (am, is, are, was, were, been), become, feel, grow, look, remain, seem, smell, sound, stay, taste**.

> The composition student is late.
> My instructor feels better.
> The ice cream tastes good.

MODIFIER IDENTIFICATION: Underline each adjective and adverb in the following sentence. Then draw an arrow to the word it modifies.

The very appreciative instructor generously gave the eager students a really high grade for their dedicated efforts toward writing improvement.

PRACTICE 11A: Choose the correct form:
1. Theodore Roosevelt said, "Speak (soft, softly) and carry a big stick."
2. Sammy Sosa was (real, really) lucky to reach second base.
3. After Waldo gave up onions, his breath improved (immense, immensely).
4. My instructor smiled (hearty, heartily) after I learned to use adverbs (correct, correctly).
5. The trainer grabbed the alligator's neck (quick, quickly).
6. The violin and piano sound (wonderful, wonderfully) together.
7. The pie smelled (delicious, deliciously) but tasted (horrible, horribly).
8. When the instructor arrived, the participants became (silent, silently) and remained (still, stilly).
9. Jim's after-shave smells (sweet, sweetly).
10. The board of directors met (recent, recently).

PRACTICE 11B: Edit the following for correct adjective/adverb usage.
1. The bride's father seemed happy as he looked happy at his new son-in-law.
2. The employees tried to talk soft, but their voices seemed loud to the facilitator.
3. Come quick to your place and sit quiet in your seat.
4. Drive slow near school playgrounds.

5. When the five o'clock bell rang loud, we quick scurried from the office.
6. The golfer's coach commented correct about her swing which looked smoothly.
7. Something in the yard smelled oddly; then the skunk appeared sudden.
8. Juliet crept to the balcony cautious and seemed calmly.
9. As Hamlet appeared unexpected in his mother's chamber, Polonius hid real quiet behind the curtain.
10. The weather outside looks frightfully, but the fire is so delightfully.

CONFUSING ADJECTIVES / ADVERBS

Good – Well

Good – an adjective which precedes a noun or follows a linking verb.

> He displays **good** skill at the keyboard.
> He is **good** at writing.
> The rain felt **good** on my burning skin.
> Olive Oyl looks **good**. (She's good-looking.)

Well –
1. adverb — indicating how action is performed
> The professor teaches **well**.
> Waldo supervises the staff **well**.

2. adjective – indicating <u>physical</u> health
> She feels **well** after her visit to her internist.
> Hilda looks **well**. (She no longer looks sick.)
> "Doctor, I don't feel **well**," said Homer.

3. to be satisfactory
> Shakespeare writes, "All's **well** that ends **well**."

Real (adjective) **Really** (adverb) / **Sure** (adjective) **Surely** (adverb)

> This seminar runs **really** smoothly.
> The instructor was **surely** right about those nasty adverbs.

PRACTICE 11C: Edit modifier usage in the following sentences:
1. She seemed to be in a real good mood while typing the essay.

2. The new computers sure cost a lot less than the old models.
3. The copy machine in the office works real good.
4. The professor was not prepared very good for the composition class.
5. Previous class records can be found easy in the updated files.
6. Dale felt he played center good, but he was also real good as a forward.
7. The ceiling in the office is deteriorating slow but sure.
8. The supervisor often gives her staff good feedback on whether their writing works good or not.

COMPARISONS OF ADJECTIVES AND ADVERBS

POSITIVE (1)	COMPARATIVE (2)	SUPERLATIVE (3 or more)
fast	faster	fastest
slow	slower	slowest
fine	finer	finest
happy	happier	happiest
careful	more (less) careful	most (least) careful
beautiful	more (less) beautiful	most (least) beautiful
good, well	better	best
little	less	least
much, many	more	most
bad	worse	worst

PRACTICE 11D: Choose the correct modifier form.
1. Jane is the (smarter, smartest) of the twins.
2. Jane is also the (faster, fastest) typist in the office.
3. He spoke (more, most) calmly to his students than Tad did.
4. Of all the replies, his was the (more, most) prompt.

PRACTICE 11E: Correct any modifier errors in the following sentences.
1. The elderly patient looks good today.
2. The instructor will respond to our writing real quick.
3. The professor responded real good to the last question.
4. The new tax form looked good to the accountant.
5. The concrete building was sure built sturdy.
6. The concrete building appears real sturdy.

7. The noon flight to North Buenie was late.
8. Report all valid results quick to the supervisor.
9. You look sharp in that new suit.
10. You should look sharp to the left and right before you turn the corner.

PRACTICE 11F: Correct any modifier errors in the following sentences.

1. Mary heard an unusual loud noise in the break room.
2. The professor looked odd at the questioning students.
3. The professor looked odd to the questioning students.
4. Gomer read the sign real slow.
5. With my sinus passage cleared, I now smell well.
6. The dandelion wine sure smells well.
7. Business is progressing as good as can be expected.
8. Kay certainly drives more careful since her fender bender.
9. Of all the coats I have tried on today, this one feels better.
10. My dad talked loud and clear when he wanted to make his point.
11. Our barn smells well.

Writing without errors doesn't make you
anything, but writing with errors—if you
give it to other people—makes you a hick,
a boob, a bumpkin" (167). – Peter Elbow (Power)

CASE OUT THE PRONOUNS

CASES OF PRONOUNS

	Nominative	Possessive	Objective
	I	my, mine	me
Singular:	you	your, yours	you
	she, he, it	her, hers, his, its	her, him, it
	we	our, ours	us
Plural:	you	your, yours	you
	they	their, theirs	them

> **Nominative Case** – subject or predicate nominative
> ***Editor's Trick: try each pronoun separately with its verb.
> **Incorrect Pronoun Usage**
> 1. Him and me were assigned to the project.

2. Mary and him came to the meeting together.

3. Have you and her had a vacation?

4. Usually David and me work together.

Predicate Nominative – a noun or pronoun that follows a linking verb (**am, is, are, was, were, be, been**). The predicate nominative refers back to the subject; therefore, if it is a pronoun, it requires the nominative case.

Correct Pronoun Usage

1. The caller was I. I was the caller. (I = caller).

2. Was the chairman he? He was the chairman. (he = chairman)

3. The receptionist who took the message was she. She was the receptionist who took the message. (she = receptionist)

4. The new students are she and I. She and I are the new students. (she and I = students)

5. The graduates were they. They were the graduates. (they = graduates)

6. The judges should have been we. We should have been the judges. (we = judges)

PRACTICE 11G: Nominative Case: Choose the correct pronoun.

1. Mr. Wright and (she, her) worked late at the office.
2. After Julia and (she, her) left, the seminar was cancelled.
3. What are you and (he, him) going to do about the missing report?
4. The winner of the award was (he, him).
5. The person who called for the appointment was (she, her).
6. Kate and (I, me) attended the writing seminar.
7. On the other hand, (he, him) and Brett did not attend.
8. I don't know if it was (he, him).
9. For our benefit, Michael and (he, him) will explain the new policy.
10. (She and I) (Her and me) took the new student to the Writing Center.
11. Are you and (they, them) writing the essay together?
12. Could it have been (he, him)?
13. It was probably (I, me) who made the error.
14. How are you and (he, him) getting to the meeting?
15. Did Jim and (she, her) leave early?

➤ **Objective Case** – direct object, indirect object, object of preposition
   ***Editor's Trick: try each pronoun separately.
      She hastily called Tom and (I, me). Called whom?
      I thanked (she, her) and (he him). Thanked whom?
      Maureen invited her sister and (we, us). Invited whom?

PRACTICE 11H: Objective Case: Choose the correct pronoun.
1. Call the receptionist and (I, me) when you find time.
2. Did you ask the doctor and (she, her) to give you a report?
3. You should remember (he and she, him and her) from last semester's class.
4. Matt will drive Paula and (she, her) to the meeting.
5. The company will call Betsy and (she, her) for an interview.
6. Tell Maxwell Smart and (he, him) about the new seminar.
7. Do you know Ellen and (she, her) through your business?
8. The manager required Homer and (I, me) to prepare an agenda.
9. Dr. Slice sent Harry and (she, her) the X-ray report.
10. We will see Hilda and (they, them) at the board meeting.
11. He stood between you and (I, me).
12. Ron worked for Mr. Handy and (he, him) for ten years.
13. Between you and (I, me), we can finish this job easily by tomorrow.
14. Tell the boss about the secretary and (he, him).
15. Have you told the CEO and (he, him) about your success yet?

➤ **Possessive Case** – ownership
   ***Possessive nouns use apostrophes. However, possessive
      pronouns never use apostrophes.
      John's report   His report
      The workers' lunch hour.   Their lunch hour.

   Incorrect Use of Possessive Case:
      This brick building is our's.
      The dog chewed on it's bone.
      Are these people friends of your's?

➤ Possessive case pronouns or nouns are used in front of a **gerund**, a
   verbal used as a noun. Gerunds end in –**ing**.
      His playing of the violin has improved.
      The dentist objected to **my** eating candy.

Your speaking to the supervisor aroused suspicion.

Her arriving late to work became a problem.

Additional Pronoun Issues:

✔ When using **than** or **as** in a comparison, complete the sentence in your mind to determine which pronoun to use.

> The captain played better than **he**. (than he played)
>
> Are you as smart as **she**? (as she is)
>
> He is nicer to Matt than **me**. (than he is to me)
>
> He is nicer to Matt than **I**. (than I am)

✔ When a pronoun is written next to the noun it refers to in **apposition**, omit the noun to decide the correct pronoun. (The **appositive** renames a noun or pronoun).

> (We, Us) mechanics service our own vehicles.
>
> The friendly host greeted (we, us) new visitors.
>
> Give the bonus to (we, us) hard-working employees.

✔ Avoid using **reflexive pronouns** (myself, himself, yourself, etc.) if another pronoun form (without –self) is suitable.

> Samson gave the best evaluations to my friend and (me, myself).
>
> My boss, my assistant, and (I, me, myself) will go to the seminar.

Note: Never use "hisself" or "theirselves"; they are considered sub-standard English words.

PRONOUN PRACTICE 11I: Correct any pronoun errors in the following sentences.

1. Mail the report to him and I.
2. She and I will be late for work.
3. The secretary asked them and she for the letters.
4. Him and the nurse filled in the patient's chart.
5. The receptionist showed the speaker and she to the main office.
6. He types better than she.
7. Us accountants registered early for the seminar.
8. The new building renovation pleased we employees.
9. She gave instructions to my colleague and myself.
10. He accidentally hit hisself with a hammer.

WHO / WHOM / WHOSE USAGE

Cases: Nominative = **who**   Objective = **whom**   Possessive = **whose**

To determine the correct form:

1. Isolate the who-whom clause.
2. Use **who** if: (a) no other subject is found, or (b) the verb is linking.
3. Use **whom** if: (a) another subject is present in the clause, and (b) the verb is action, not linking.

Examples:

The new manager, (who, whom) has taken Mr. Wright's position, came from Texas.

The new manager, (who, whom) I met today, came from Texas.

Does anyone know (who, whom) the new manager is?

PRACTICE 11J: Who / Whom: Select the proper form.

1. (Who, Whom) came first?
2. The paper machine operator is (who, whom)?
3. (Who, Whom) shall I send to control the flow of materials into the print center office?
4. (Who, Whom) do you think will operate the computer in our office?
5. Everybody (who, whom) received an invitation will attend the school picnic.
6. The writers (who, whom) I most admire are those who take the time to revise and edit.
7. If we had known (who, whom) the writer was, we would have explained the assignment more carefully.
8. The union officers will be (whoever, whomever) the committee nominates.
9. Send the job application to (whoever, whomever) applies first.
10. (Who, Whom) do you want to win the World Series?

PRACTICE 11K: All Pronoun Usage. Correct any pronoun errors.

1. She is the person whom, I believe, should be promoted.
2. Kathy and me qualified for a big raise.
3. It was them.
4. The company policy regarding absenteeism was written by the CEO and he.

5. Us office personnel will help the custodian clean out the basement.
6. Did you let Hortense use your key to the lounge?
7. Mr. Wright will give you and she another chance to do the job.
8. The new student is whom?
9. Ruth and her are trying to coordinate their rides to campus.
10. Neither Ed nor them can complete their portfolios until next summer.
11. A dispute arose between their consultant and they.
12. To whom did you and her give the keys to my office?

PRACTICE 11L: All Pronoun Usage. Correct any pronoun errors.

1. Us participants can write letters in our sleep.
2. Them and their assistants keep the office running smoothly.
3. Are us colleagues invited to the professors' banquet?
4. Show Carol and me the new computer system.
5. Working in the tax division usually relaxes Doyle and I.
6. I do not appreciate him messing with my computer.
7. Waldo knows whom the boss really is.
8. Mr. Smith, who hired me today, is the new branch manager.
9. It couldn't have been them.
10. The administrative assistants and myself will go out for lunch.
11. Somebody, either Waldo or him, answered the phone.
12. Have you seen Bridget or she yet?

CHAPTER 12

"Good MECHANICS Keep Writing Motors Running Smoothly."

"Ninety percent of writers can use the comma correctly 75% of the time. But only one percent of writers can use the comma correctly 99 percent of the time" (132).
—Brandon Royal

COMMA PLACEMENT

In addition to dates and addresses, place commas in sentences in three situations –**introductory** elements, **interrupting** elements, or **intertwining** elements.

> ➤ **INTRODUCTORY**   Word, Phrase, Clause

Word**,** SENTENCE.

Yes, sentence.

Oh, sentence.

No, sentence.

Well, sentence.

Phrase**,** SENTENCE. (phrase = group of words without subject or predicate)

1. Prepositional Phrase – "Clue words."

The following list includes some commonly used prepositions:

among	between	on	up
around	during	over	with
as well as	from	through	within
at	in	to	without
behind	of	toward	
below	off	under	

Examples of Prepositional Phrases:
over the river   through the woods   to Grandmother's house

2. Participle Phrase
- Present Participle (-ing) –

Driving down the highway at a moderate speed, Waldo was able
to avoid the crossing deer.
- Past Participle (-ed, -en, -d, -t) –

Written for composition class, the essay drew rave reviews.
- Present Perfect (Having + past participle) –

Having selected a topic, Fritz began writing his essay.

Clause, **SENTENCE.** (clause = groups of words containing a subject
and predicate)

Adverb Clause "Clue Words":
The following words commonly begin an adverb clause:

although	even though	unless	where
as	if	until	wherever
because	once	when	while
before	since	whenever	

Note: No comma is required when these clause "clue words" appear
after the main clause.

Examples of Adverb Clauses:
When the moon comes over the mountain
As time goes by

COMMA PRACTICE 12A: Place commas in the following
sentences.

1. Oh I almost forgot today's seminar.
2. In my opinion commas can confuse even the best writers.
3. Expecting the worst we planned for the project.
4. Tripped in the hallway by Ralph Jim was carried to the doctor's office.
5. Before the half the Packers jogged into the locker room.
6. After the game ended the Hawks had won again.
7. Because writing is challenging I must put forth good effort.
8. Harry are you chilly on top?
9. Typing for only ten minutes Hilda finished the forty-five page essay.
10. If students study hard they usually do well in college.

11. Having studied for only ten minutes Waldo approached the quiz apprehensively.
12. While the Cubs lose the Cardinals continue to win.

COMMA PRACTICE 12B:
1. Compose a sentence with an <u>introductory word</u>.

2. Compose a sentence with an <u>introductory phrase</u>.

3. Compose a sentence with an <u>introductory clause</u>.

Regarding the comma, "When in doubt, leave it out." — Mark Twain

➢ **INTERRUPTING Word, Phrase, Clause**

SEN, interrupting word**, TENCE.**
> John, too, writes well.
> I feel, Tom, that you write well. (Direct Address)

SEN, interrupting phrase**, TENCE**
> Eldred, on the other hand, struggles with his writing.
> Homer, in my opinion, writes like Hemingway.
> This, my dear friend, presents quite a challenge. (Direct Address)
> > **Appositive** – renames or describes:
> Ralph, my older brother, earns the bucks in our family.
> My toughest class, Advanced Nuclear Trigonometry, presents quite a challenge.

SEN, interrupting clause**, TENCE.**
> (Clue Words: **who, whom, which, where, whose**)

<u>Non-restrictive</u>—adds interesting or useful information but is not necessary for meaning. Set it off with commas so readers see it as helpful but not essential information.
> Walter, who teaches at NICC, writes well enough to be published.

Walter, who teaches at NICC, loves to write poetry.

Walter, whom I admire, teaches at NICC.

Walter's latest poem, which I love, uses a great deal of imagery.

Restrictive—adds essential information; <u>not</u> set it off with commas so that readers see it as a necessary part of the sentence. Because *that* can specify rather than simply add information, its clause usually requires no commas.

The poem that I need to search for is written by Robert Frost.

COMMA PRACTICE 12C: Place commas in the following sentences.

1. Kay too teaches elementary students.
2. Shakespeare my favorite dramatist wrote 37 wonderful plays.
3. Yes Herman you have a bad case of halitosis.
4. Bob Hope a terrific comedian instilled laughter into the hearts of most Americans.
5. Early computers large and immobile have been replaced by smaller models.
6. Kay my lovely wife teaches third grade.
7. Mr. Ed who talked like a human ate like a horse.
8. Buenie where I was raised looks like a pimple on the large cheek of Iowa.
9. My dad whom I greatly respected placed a fair and valid curfew on his sons.
10. My brother the thinker in the family earns more money than I.
11. Karen Morris who was offered four scholarships will attend NICC this fall.
12. The computer working quickly and accurately processed useful information.

COMMA PRACTICE 12D:

1. Compose a sentence with an <u>interrupting word</u>.

2. Compose a sentence with an <u>interrupting phrase</u>.

3. Compose a sentence with an <u>interrupting clause</u>.

➢ **INTERTWINING – joins words, phrases, clauses, sentences.**
> **Series** (list) of words, phrases, clauses. (Use one less comma.)
>> I enjoy baseball, basketball, football, and golf. (words)
>> I love playing the piano, attending concerts, writing essays, and eating pizza. (phrases)
>> I enjoy a picnic when the weather feels warm, when the sky looks clear, and when the food is provided. (clauses)

> **Mini-Series:**
>> That secretary is a competent, personable professional.

Compound Sentence: SENTENCE, conjunction SENTENCE.
> "Glue Words": **for, and, nor, but, or, yet, so (FANBOYS)**
>> Gene has washed his old car, and he hopes to attract a buyer.
>> Our former boss demanded a high standard of work, but our new boss favors quantity over quality.
>> We can stay home and eat lamb, or we can go out for pizza.

Compound Sentence: SENTENCE; word, SENTENCE.
> "Glue Words":

	...; additionally, ...	...; also, ...
...; consequently, ...	...; furthermore ,...	...; however, ...	...; indeed, ...
...still, ...	...; then, ...	...; therefore, ...	...; thus, ...

>> Gene has washed his old car; therefore, he hopes to attract a buyer.
>> Our former boss demanded a high standard of work; however, our new boss favors quantity over quality.
>> We can stay home and eat lamb; then, we could go out for pizza.

Compound Sentence: SENTENCE; SENTENCE.
>> Gene has washed his old car; he hopes to attract a buyer.
>> Our former boss demanded a high standard of work; our new boss favors quantity over quality.
>> We can stay home and eat lamb; we could go out for pizza.

PRACTICE 12E: Use commas and/or semi-colons to punctuate the following sentences.
1. I visualize a quiet relaxing pleasant and peaceful office.
2. She liked the manager when he was kind when he was patient and when he left the office.
3. Our computer expert acted fairly smart but sometimes he suffered from an e-mail virus.
4. The eighty-year-old couple were married they spent their honeymoon on the mountain slopes of Vail.
5. I need to earn some extra money therefore I teach some extra classes.
6. The instructor stumbled into the classroom bumped into the desk kicked a chair and laughed in relief.
7. Most of us loved the seminar but Zeke considered it boring.
8. We worked on the letter for hours then handed it to the supervisor.
9. I put in long hours at my job yet I could do even more.
10. Joe does not fear snakes nor do turtles frighten him.
11. You must honor the office policies or suffer the consequences.

PRACTICE 12F:
1. Compose a sentence containing a SERIES of <u>words</u>, <u>phrases</u>, or <u>clauses</u>.

2. Compose a COMPOUND SENTENCE with a conjunction (FANBOYS).

3. Compose a COMPOUND SENTENCE without a conjunction (use semi-colon).

DATES & ADDRESSES   Use a comma to separate items in dates and addresses.
      DATES: Use a comma between the day of the month and the year and also after the year when it does not end the sentence.

Do not use a comma between the month and the day. Do not use a comma when only the month and the year are used.

ADDRESSES: Consider the street number and street name as one item and the state and zip code as one item. Each additional item is followed by a comma. No comma is used between the state and the zip code.

> I was born on July 19, 1947, at Mercy Hospital in Dubuque, Iowa 52002.
>
> I was born at Mercy Hospital in Dubuque, Iowa, on July 19, 1947.

PRACTICE 12G: Write a sentence that tells the date and location of your birth.

PRACTICE 12H: Comma Usage Analyze the passage, and place commas as needed. Above each comma, place the corresponding number from the list below to designate its usage in the passage.

1 - introductory word	4 – interrupting word	7 – intertwining series
2 - introductory phrase	5 – interrupting phrase	8 – compound sent.
3 – introductory clause	6 – interrupting clause	9 – date or address

Professor I.M. Snoring had spent countless hours researching his area of expertise advanced microscopic photosynthesis. He was planning a lecture for his 8 AM class the following Monday. After many hours in the library Professor Snoring had accumulated a large stack of notes. He then organized them in outline form and he placed them in a three-ring binder. The professor was pleased with his work and anxiously awaited the opportunity to share his expertise with his class.

When the night before the lecture arrived Professor Snoring stayed up late into the evening reviewing his notes. After about five hours of study he grew tired and decided to get some rest. At 6:30 AM he heard his alarm go off and he immediately jumped out of bed. He brushed his teeth put on his best sweater and ate his Corn Flakes. In an eager frame of mind he hopped on his Honda motorcycle and headed for his office.

Although the traffic slowed him a bit Professor Snoring arrived at the campus in good time found a spot close to his office and tied his motorcycle to a tree. He briskly walked to his office and unlocked the door. On the floor he found a letter from his brother Waldo who lived at 1032 High Lane Filmore Iowa which was dated May 1 2003. Waldo who was born three years before the professor farmed 380 acres just off Highway 151. In the letter Waldo said he was planning a vacation trip to Millville Iowa and hoped the professor would join him. Professor Snoring decided to respond to the request at a later time.

Then Professor Snoring left for his eagerly anticipated 8 AM lecture. The students groggily entered the lecture hall after their long weekend. The professor began his lecture as late-comers continued to straggle in one by one but that did not derail the professor's speech. After one hour and fourteen minutes of non-stop lecture the professor finally looked up from his notes to find numerous listeners fast asleep. The professor became undone halted his lecture picked out a student in the back of the room and said "Say John would you please wake up that student who is sleeping in the seat next to you?"

In reply the startled John stammered "You wake him up yourself Professor Snoring. You put him to sleep."

PRACTICE 12I: OVERALL PRACTICE: Compose sentences to fit each of the patterns listed below. Edit punctuation carefully.

1. Introductory word

2. Introductory phrase

3. Introductory clause

4. Interrupting word

5. Interrupting phrase

6. Interrupting clause

7. Series of words, phrases, or clauses

8. Compound with conjunction (**FANBOYS**)

9. Compound without conjunction (semi-colon)

10. Compound-complex

11. Date and Address

APOSTROPHE

1. Add an apostrophe and an <u>s</u> to form the possessive of a singular noun, of a plural noun not ending in <u>s</u>, and an indefinite pronoun.

the man's car	the witness's responses	
the boss's office	Mary's desk	(singular nouns)

| the men's glee club | the women's coat room | (plural nouns) |
| the children's choir | the people's opinions | |

| anybody's game | everyone's future | (indefinite |
| someone's work | nobody's fault | pronouns) |

Note: add an apostrophe alone to "hard to pronounce" singular words.
        Miss Phillips' election   Moses' laws   Euripides' plays

2. Add only an apostrophe to form the possessive of a plural noun ending in s.

the bosses' cars   ladies' coat room   attorneys' offices   (plural nouns)

PRACTICE 12J: Make the following examples possessive.

a. today _____ assignments   b. boss _____ tirade
c. job _____ pressures   d. workers ____ duties
e. attorney _____ fees   f. attorneys _____ parking lot
g. men _____ basketball league   h. anybody_____ guess

3. Possessive pronouns (my, his, hers, its, ours, yours, theirs) never require an apostrophe to show possession.

        The victory is ours. (not our's)   The dog chased its tail. (not it's)
                        Remember: it's = it is.

4. The last word takes 's to show possession in compound nouns, names of business firms, and two nouns showing joint ownership.

| father-in-law's profession | mother-in-law's cooking | (compound |
| brother-in-law's job | Attorney General's statement | nouns) |

| Sears Roebuck's insurance plan | |
| Honkamp Krueger's employees | (business firms) |

| Tom and Geri's cat | Mom and Dad's car | (joint possession) |

Note: Place 's after each item if you want to show individual possession.

    Tom's and Geri's cats   Mom's and Dad's cars

5. Add 's to form the plurals of certain signs, numbers, letters, and words.

four t's and two s's	all 6's and 7's
14 and's in the letter	too many which's in writing

6. Use an apostrophe in a contraction to show that letters or figures are left out.

has not = hasn't	is not = isn't
they are = they're	class of 1988 = class of '88
it is = it's	

PRACTICE 12K: Add apostrophes as needed.

a. Stephen King and John Grisham novels
b. Tom, Dick, and Harry project
c. four –s and four –i in Mississippi
d. Rodgers and Hammerstein *The King and I*
e. Tom, Dick, and Harry bikes (each own a bike)
f. Its time for the secretarial staff to take its' coffee break.
g. Dont snore.

PRACTICE 12L: Add or delete apostrophes in the following sentences.

1. Womens' lib grows stronger because of it's forceful position.
2. The girls choir will sing for the mens glee club.
3. Weve won the clients confidence.
4. Before Fridays rain, Charleys goat ate eight acre's of grass and felt an ache in its stomach.
5. My mother-in-laws cooking has become famous in three states'.
6. When your editing you're drafts, check carefully to dot your is and cross your ts.

PRACTICE 12M: Provide the correct possessive forms in the following paragraph:

The students essays show good use of the writing process. Student writers revision strategies have been used effectively. Everyones focus on improving his or her writing style is encouraging. Each students editing is also improving. Strunk and Whites book, *Elements of Style*, seems to be helping all the writers knowledge of style. People from miles around Peosta will flock to read the students wonderful writings.

SEMI-COLONS

1. Use a semi-colon between two sentences to form a compound sentence without a coordinating conjunction or with a transitional word such as *consequently, furthermore, however, instead, otherwise, then, therefore.*

> Writers must practice their craft; they will then see improvement in time.
>
> Writers must practice their craft; otherwise, they will not see improvement.

2. Use a semi-colon between items in a series (list) containing internal punctuation.

> In the literature class, the students read *Things Fall Apart*, an African novel; *Madame Bovary*, a French novel; *Wuthering Heights*, a British novel; and *Antigone*, a Greek drama.

COLONS

1. Use a colon after a preceding complete sentence to introduce a list, a quotation, or an appositive.

> My typical day includes the following: an early breakfast, two morning classes, two afternoon classes, reading interesting essays, walking for exercise, a hearty supper, and a good night's sleep.
>
> Analyze this passage from *Henry IV, Part I* by Shakespeare: "What is honor? A word. What is in that word "honor"? What is that "honor"? Air…Honor is a mere scutcheon" (5.1.133-140).
>
> Students should now recognize the syntactical meaning of the compound sentence: two independent clauses joined by comma and conjunction or by a semi-colon.

2. Use a colon after the salutation of a formal letter, between hours and minutes, to show ratios, between title and subtitle, between chapter and verse of Biblical references, and between city and publisher in reference entries.

> Dear Professor Wright: 9:20 a.m. (or AM)
>
> The ratio of students to teacher is 11:1.
>
> *Teaching and Performing: Ideas for Energizing Your Classes*
>
> 1 Corinthians 13:1-13   Dubuque, IA: McGraw-Hill

DASHES
(Type two hyphens with no space before or after them.)
1. Use dashes for emphasis and to set off appositives that contain commas.

Everything I touched today—my car, my computer, my TV, my stove—all broke down in seconds.

PARENTHESES
1. Use parentheses to enclose brief explanations or interruptions.

After serving her husband his normal breakfast (bacon, eggs, hash browns, toast, fruit, coffee, juice), Mildred went back to bed.

2. Use parentheses around letters or numbers labeling items in a series.

The portfolio should contain the following items: (1) an introduction, (2) an example of a full process, (3) revised essays, (4) entry slip reflections, (5) a diagnostic essay, (6) personal inclusions, and (7) a metacognitive conclusion.

ITALICS / UNDERLINE
1. Italicize or underline the titles of magazines, newspapers, pamphlets, books, plays, films, radio and television programs, book-length poems, ballets, operas, long musical compositions, record albums, CD's, legal cases, and names of ships or aircraft.

Newsweek (magazine)   *Telegraph Herald* (newspaper)
Macbeth (play)   Walden (book)
Field of Dreams (film)   Cheers (TV Program)

Do not italicize, underline, or use quotation marks around titles of religious works.

Bible   Koran   Ten Commandments   Torah

2. Italicize or underline foreign words used in an English sentence.

The students became accustomed to Professor Wright's *modus operandi*.

END PUNCTUATION
1. Use periods to end statements and commands.

This writing seminar requires lots of writing and thinking.

Turn in all written reports on Thursday.

Note: use periods in abbreviations. Do not add a second period if the sentence ends with a period indicating an abbreviation.

Mr. Mrs. Ms. Dr. B.A. M.A. Ph.D. R.N. B.C. A.D.

Ms. Jones recently completed her course work for her Ph.D.

2. Use a question mark following a direct question.

How many participants have completed the writing assignment?

3. Avoid using exclamation points in business and professional writing. The wording should show the emotion.

QUOTATION MARKS

1. Use quotation marks for titles of songs, poems, short stories, lectures, courses, chapters of books, and articles in newspapers, magazines, or encyclopedias.

"On Top of Ol' Smokey" (song)

"Young Goodman Brown" (short story)

"Cultures Through Literature" (course)

"The Road Not Taken" (poem)

2. Place punctuation used with quotation marks as follows:

a. Place a comma or a period <u>inside</u> closing quotation marks.

"Good prose," suggests Somerset Maughan, "should resemble the conversation of a well-bred man."

b. Place a colon or semi-colon <u>outside</u> closing quotation marks.

Professor Wright stated, "You have passed this course"; what he said after that I was too astonished to hear.

In the words of Professor Wright, the following writers have "exceeded my expectations": Norrie North, Samuel South, Erica East, and Walter West.

c. Place a question mark or exclamation point inside the closing quotation marks when it is part of the quotation.

"Are the peer response groups finished yet?" inquired the composition instructor.

d. Place a question mark or exclamation point outside the closing quotation marks when it is part of the entire sentence.

Have you read Frost's poem "The Road Not Taken"?

CAPITALIZATION

1. Capitalize the first word of a sentence and the first word of a direct quotation.

When the instructor requested the assignment, Herman muttered, "My dog ate it."

2. Capitalize proper nouns and adjectives:

Specific Individuals   Michael Jordan   William Shakespeare

Specific Places & Geographical Areas   Pacific Ocean   Europe

Institutions, Organizations, Government Departments
>   the Supreme Court   Northeast Iowa Community College
>   St. Louis Cardinals

Historical Events, Documents, Periods
>   the Renaissance   the French and Indian War
>   the Bill of Rights

Days of the Week, Months, Holidays
>   Monday   May   Father's Day

Religions and Sacred Terms
>   Allah   Christian   Zeus   the Bible

Races, Nationalities, and Languages
>   Caucasians   Arabs   Irish

Trade names   Banana Republic   Toyota   HyVee

Titles preceding, but not after, a proper name
>   President Mark Smith   Mark Smith, our president
>   Professor Waldo Wright   Waldo Wright, my professor

Titles of books, articles, plays, films, songs, stories, poems, essays, paintings
>   Tom Sawyer   "The Star Spangled Banner"

> *"Concentrate on the mundane housekeeping jobs,*
> *like fixing misspellings and picking up inconsistencies.*
> *There'll be plenty; only God gets it right the first time*
> *and only a slob says, 'Oh, well, let it go, that's what*
> *copyeditors are for'" (212).* – Stephen King

SPELLING

1. Write i before e except after c or when sounded like a as in neighbor and weigh.
>   receive   ceiling   brief   relief   believe   eight

2. If a word (sit) ends in a consonant (t) preceded by a vowel (i), double the final consonant before adding a suffix which begins with a vowel (sitting).
>   admit = admitted   slam = slammed   occur = occurring

3. If a word ends in a silent e, drop the e before adding a suffix that begins with a vowel.
>   come+ing = coming   write+ing = writing
>   debate+able = debatable

When *y* is the last letter of a word preceded by a consonant, change *y* to *i* before adding a suffix—except those suffixes beginning with *i*.

> hurry = hurried   lady = ladies
> happy = happiness   beauty = beautiful

Note: when forming the plural of a word that ends in y preceded by a vowel, add s.

> play = plays   donkey = donkeys

4. Spell out numbers from zero through nine and all numbers that begin sentences. Use digits for numbers 10 and above and for ages.

> No — 5 cars entered the parking ramp.
> Yes – Five cars entered the parking ramp.
> No – 2004 was the year the Red Sox won the World Series.
> Yes – In 2004, the Red Sox won the World Series.
> No — Stanley has fifteen siblings.
> Yes — Stanley has 15 siblings.
> No – At age eleven, Stanley wrote a book.
> Yes – At age 11, Stanley wrote a book.
> Consult a reputable dictionary for variations and exceptions.

CHAPTER 13

Job Seeking Skills

"I found that the men and women who got to the top
were those who did the jobs they had in hand,
with everything they had of energy and
enthusiasm and hard work."
—Harry S. Truman

Securing a job can seem like a daunting venture, so this chapter offers practical tips for seeking employment in a position that interests you and fits your background and skills. The job search may seem less intimidating and more manageable if it is divided into stages, such as

Job search

Cover letter

Resume

Interviewing strategies

Follow-up.

JOB SEARCH

Analyze your skills, interests, abilities, and goals to determine what type of job suits you best. Then begin your job search. You can find job listings in many different ways. You might network or communicate with people you know who might connect you with jobs available in your area of interest and location. These contacts might include family members, friends, employees already working in the field, former professors in your major field of study, anyone who might suggest job availability. Networking may send you to another lead and another and so on.

Besides networking, you might use the internet. Various search engines, such as Google or Yahoo, can lead you to job availability. The challenge with internet searches may be limiting your search. Searching for "accountants," for example, could lead to thousands and thousands of hits, which would require endless time to sort through. Therefore, try to limit and specify the position you seek and the general location if you choose to search the internet.

An excellent source of job availability is located in your school's career-development office. Most colleges designate a job placement coordinator/counselor, who collects and posts job opportunities submitted to the career-placement office. Many local and national businesses, companies, industries, health facilities, and government agencies will send career-placement offices information concerning job openings. Many placement offices post jobs on a bulletin board in a prominent location at the college. In addition, most colleges now post the job opportunities on-line at the college's web-site location. So even if you graduated years ago, your college may offer you a good source of new employment opportunities.

Newspaper classified sections offer job listings, as well. Larger newspapers offer daily listings of jobs available in the "help-wanted" section. However, the most extensive lists are available in the Sunday editions of local and national newspapers. Some businesses, companies, and industries will even take out classified ads in order to attract perspective employees.

Yet another job source might be job fairs. These job fairs are usually advertised on the internet, via college placement offices, in newspaper ads, or through local workforce development agencies. Job fairs offer employers and job seekers the opportunity to contact each other in one setting and visit face-to-face on one specified date and time.

In addition, the yellow pages of your local phone book contain a listing of employment agencies. These agencies can help you locate job opportunities and offer counseling in applying for jobs. Some of these agencies offer free services while others charge pre-established fees for their services.

Like any worthwhile venture, the more time and effort you put into seeking job opportunities, the more chances may come your way. So, use any and all available means to locate job possibilities that seem to suit and interest you. Once you locate the jobs you are interested in, you need to move to the next stage, contacting the business or organization by means of a cover letter and resume. The next section offers suggestions on developing productive cover letters and resumes that bring positive results to your job search.

PRACTICE 13A: LOCATE A JOB. Using whatever means available—the internet, newspapers, local job service agencies, networking—locate a job of interest to you. Write a minimum three-paragraph description of the job, including all pertinent information you might need to apply for that position.

COVER LETTER

The cover letter offers you the opportunity of introducing yourself to a perspective employer and provides your means of "getting your foot in the door." The cover letter does not guarantee a job, or even an interview. This introductory correspondence may simply get you the opportunity to move to the next step—the interview. You need to focus intently on good writing skills in composing your cover letter because they serve as your initial introduction to the employer. The letter must make a good impression and show your ability to communicate clearly and correctly in writing so that you achieve your initial goal, the opportunity to be interviewed.

The cover letter lets the employer hear your voice via your writing. The letter will reflect your personality, your interest in the job and the company, your attention to detail, your communication skills, and your intelligence. So, design each cover letter for the specific job you are seeking and put forth the necessary time and focus to make the letter the best possible correspondence you can write. Remember the goal of this letter: why should the employer select you to be invited for an interview above others applying for the job?

- **Prewriting Considerations**
    (1) Get the specific individual's name who will conduct your job placement. Finding the name and position may require some research or a direct call to the company. Never address a cover letter "To Whom It May Concern" or "Dear Sir or Madame."
    (2) Research the company. Use the internet to determine the organization's goals, concerns, problems, and particular aspects of the position.
    (3) Make a list of the items you need to include in the letter.
    (4) In composing your cover letter, you need to focus intently on good writing skills because they serve as your initial introduction to the employer.
    (5) Word process each letter and edit it carefully.

- **Contents of the Cover Letter**

    Your letter should attract attention. Use a conversational, respectful, professional tone. Avoid starchy, "brainiac" word choices that make you seem phony or pretentious. Be concise and to the point. Get into the letter, state your case, and get out. Employers do not have time nor want to read long, drawn out letters. Indicate why you are interested in the job, explain how you might fit into the company, and indicate how you qualify for the position. Stress your achievements confidently without sounding boastful, and try to refer your reader to your resume for more detailed information. Compose the cover letter in paragraph form and **EDIT CAREFULLY.**

- **Cover Letter Format**

Your Street Address
City, State Zip
e-mail address
date

Name of Employer
His/Her Title
Company/Organization
Street Address
City, State Zip

Dear (Mr., Ms., Dr…):

The opening paragraph should be brief—three to four sentences—and should attract reader attention. State the purpose of your letter, indicating the position you are applying for. Indicate how you learned about the position. Indicate why you are interested in the position. Name any personal contact you may have in or with the company.

The body of your letter may range from one to four paragraphs. Indicate what talents and experiences qualify you for the job. Be as specific as possible, and refer your reader to your resume for more details. Indicate what assets you bring to the company rather than what the company can do for you. Confidently sell yourself without boasting by emphasizing your key qualifications. List specific information that will attract the employer's attention so that he or she will want to invite you for an interview.

The closing paragraph is used to request an interview. Inform the reader when, where, and how you may be reached. If the employer is located a great distance, you might suggest an initial phone interview. Express your anticipation of meeting for an interview. Finally, close with a positive, sincere expression of gratitude for the reader's time and consideration.

Sincerely,

(Sign your name in ink)

Type your name

Enclosure: resume

SAMPLE COVER LETTER

4321 Riverside Drive
North Buena Vista, IA 52066
October 12, 2007

Mr. I. N. Charge
Chief Executive Officer
Smooth Tire Company
10502 Market Rd.
Peosta, IA 52068

Dear Mr. Charge:

I am writing to apply for the position of controller in your Accounting Department at Smooth Tire Company. I learned of the opening from your Administrative Assistant, Silvia Shrimp, and I also saw your ad in last Sunday's Telegraph Herald classified section. I have completed my Master's Degree in Accounting and am very interested in the controller position at Smooth Tire Company.

I have worked in the accounting field throughout my professional career, and I bring extensive and practical knowledge and experience to the position. I feel I can add significant expertise and professionalism to the Smooth Tire Company and assist its continued growth and success. I have enclosed a copy of my resume, which details my professional and educational background.

I would be delighted to meet with you to discuss the open position in accounting. If you wish to arrange an interview, please contact me at the address listed above or by phone at 563.345.7809. Thank you for your time and consideration, and I look forward to hearing from you in the near future.

Sincerely,

Ann Betteryet

Ann Betteryet

Enclosure: resume

- **Cover Letter Proofreading**

EDIT CAREFULLY. Your cover letter must be grammatically perfect. Use the spell check and grammar check on your computer. Then ask a friend or family member (preferably an English major) to edit your letter. Then ask another friend(s) or family member(s) to proofread the letter. The more readers you get to critique your letter the better, and the more likely all revisions and corrections will be identified and adjusted.

PRACTICE 13B: COVER LETTER.   Write a cover letter to the business/organization that you located and researched for PRACTICE 13A and that could be adapted for future employment opportunities. **EDIT CAREFULLY.**

RESUME

The resume's purpose, as with the cover letter, is to "get your foot in the door," to get an interview. The resume highlights your qualifications, education, experiences, skills, and accomplishments. Employers seldom spend more than about one minute browsing a resume, so limit the resume to one page, two maximum if you have extensive work experience. To prepare your resume, take time to pre-write by making a list of those significant aspects of your background and experience that will help sell yourself. Write your resume by using action verbs where possible and avoiding first person "I." For example, write "Administrative Assistant" rather than "I was a secretary." Or, write "Promoted to Assistant Manager in March 2007" rather than "I was promoted to Assistant Manager in March 2007."

Do not include personal items like age, height, weight, health issues, family size unless they might influence your job performance or make you stand out among the candidates for the position. Also, do not include any items pertaining to salary on your resume.

Use 8.5x11-inch, white or off-white paper. Print on one side only in a font size no smaller than 10 and no larger than 14, with 12 point font being standard. Choose one type face, such as Times New Roman, throughout. Avoid italics or underlining, graphics, or shading. Do not fold or staple your resume. If you mail your resume, send it in a large envelope. And remember, **EDIT CAREFULLY.**

Contents of a Resume

- ## Heading

     At the top of your resume in the center of the page, list your name, address, permanent telephone number, cell-phone number, and e-mail address. Avoid nicknames. If you are a graduating student or plan to relocate in the near future, consider using your parents' address or a friend's permanent address.

- ## Employee Objective (optional)

     The objective informs the employer of the type of position you are seeking. If you choose to include an objective, be specific and revise it for each separate job and employer you send the resume to.

- ## Education

     New graduates should list educational information before work experience. If you have significant work experience, place that section before educational information. List your most recent educational information first. Include your degree, major, institution attended, and any minor degrees, if applicable. Add any significant academic honors. Do not list high school information unless it is relevant and recent or if you wish to highlight a specific honor or award that would enhance your qualifications. Also, consider adding any internships or study abroad programs that need to be emphasized.

- ## Work Experience

     Provide an overview of your work experiences that enhance your qualifications. List your most recent job first and work in reverse order to your first, relevant job. If you have little full-time experience, list part-time, temporary, or intern positions you've held. Provide the title of the position, the name of the organization and its location (city, state), and dates of employment. Then use action verbs to describe the specific responsibilities and achievements the job entailed.

- ## Special Skills (optional)

     You may choose to add special skills or competencies, such as computer or writing skills, leadership experience, volunteer organizations, professional affiliations, publications, presentations, or pertinent activities that can enhance your qualifications for employment. Be judicious here. Do not repeat information provided elsewhere, and include only information pertinent to the specific job you are seeking.

- **References**

Obtain permission from people you wish to serve as your references. Your references should be personally acquainted with you and should know your character, qualifications, and abilities. Former employers, professors or teachers, or colleagues you've worked with can serve as excellent references. However, do not identify your references on your resume. Otherwise, the perspective employer may contact them before you have the opportunity to sell yourself. Rather, write "References furnished on request." Then prepare a handout with your references' names, positions, addresses, and phone numbers to present to the employer upon request. As a courtesy, contact your references when you find a job and thank them for their assistance.

- **Resume Proofreading**

EDIT CAREFULLY. Your resume must be grammatically perfect. Use the spell check and grammar check on your computer. Then ask a friend or family member (preferable an English major) to edit your resume. Then ask another friend(s) or family member(s) to proofread the resume. The more readers you get to critique your resume the better, and the more likely all revisions and corrections will be identified and adjusted.

SAMPLE RESUMES

RESUME FOR RECENT GRADUATE

I.M. Superb
2436 Jupiter Lane
North Buena Vista, IA 52066
563.345.0987
isuperb@bigfoot.com

Objective	To secure a permanent position in the accounting profession.
Education	BA in Accounting, University of Iowa, May 2007
	AAS Accounting Specialist, Northeast Iowa Community College, May 2005
Honors	Graduated Cum Laude from the University of Iowa
	Dean's List — University of Iowa—four semesters
	Dean's List — Northeast Iowa Community College—four semesters
	Listed in Who's Who Among College Students — 2006, 2007
	Member of Phi Theta Kappa Educational Fraternity, Northeast Iowa Community College Chapter
	Member of Student Senate — Northeast Iowa Community College
Experience	Mars Accounting Firm, P.C., Intern—spring semester, 2007
	Calculated individual client's tax forms
	Assisted in corporate tax preparation
	Assisted in inventory records
	Assisted in payroll
Special Skills	Experienced in using IBM AS/400 system, computer spreadsheets, database, and Asset Accounting Program
References	Furnished on request

RESUME FOR AN EXPERIENCED APPLICANT

Ann Betteryet
4321 Riverside Drive
North Buena Vista, IA 52066
563.345.7809
ambetter@hotmail.com

Objective	To secure a position as controller in a major corporation.
Experience	Controller/MIS Director, Tear Motors, Sadbrook, IA, 2004-present
	Controller/MIS Director, Hot Seat Furniture, Bed Rock, WI, 2002-2004
	Accountant, Buenie Accountants Unlimited, North Buena Vista, IA, 2001-2002
Education	MA in Accounting, University of Northern Iowa, May 2006
	BA in Accounting, University of Iowa, May 2007
	AAS Accounting Specialist, Northeast Iowa Community College, May 2005
Honors	Northeast Iowa Accountant of the Year, 2006
	Listed in Who's Who Among America's Business Leaders
	Graduated Cum Laude from the University of Iowa
	Dean's List — University of Iowa—four semesters
	Dean's List — Northeast Iowa Community College— four semesters
	Listed in Who's Who Among College Students – 1998, 1999
	Member of Phi Theta Kappa Educational Fraternity, Northeast Iowa Community College Chapter
	Member of Student Senate — Northeast Iowa Community College
Special Skills	Experienced in using IBM AS/400 system, computer spreadsheets, database, and Asset Accounting
References	Furnished on request

PRACTICE 13C: RESUME Create a workable resume for the position that you located and that could be adapted for future employment opportunities. **EDIT CAREFULLY.**

INTERVIEWING STRATEGIES

Presuming your cover letter and resume have served their purposes, you are now ready to interview for a position you sought. Remember that the interview is a two-way proposition. You are being evaluated, but at the same time, you are evaluating the job and the people who are offering it. An initial interview process may consist of one 30 minute conference, or it may last longer. Also, depending on the first interview, you may re-called for a second, and possibly more, longer interview(s)—a positive sign you are being considered for the position. Furthermore, the interview may involve one interviewer or a panel of interviewers. Depending on distance constraints, some first interviews are conducted via phone or teleconference with subsequent interview sessions face-to-face. Most of the time, the method of the interview will be unknown ahead of time, so you need to prepare as well as possible for any interview scenario.

- **Prior to the Interview**
  Learn everything you can about the organization before the interview. Consult the Internet, literature about the company, or even current employees. Try to determine information like the size of the company, its history, its sales volume, its product rating, it plans for new products or services, and its future plans for growth or expansion. If you cannot find information that you deem important, ask your interviewer(s) during the interview, which will also show your interest in the company and your preparation for the interview. The more you know about the company in advance, the better you are likely to do in the interview.

  Try to anticipate questions which may come up in the interview by writing them down. The following are frequently asked general interview questions:
  1. Tell us something about yourself.
  2. What is your greatest accomplishment so far in your life?
  3. Why are you interested in this position?
  4. What are your short and long-term career goals?
  5. Why are you leaving your present position (or last position)?

6. What strengths do you bring to this position?
7. What weaknesses do you bring to this position?
8. Where do you expect to see yourself in five years, in ten years?
9. Describe your work habits. Do you work better alone or with others?
10. What do you do for relaxation? What do you do for professional development?
11. Tell us about a challenging problem you encountered in your last job and how you handled it?
12. Why should we hire you for this position?
13. Do you have any questions for us (the interviewers)? Having questions prepared to ask the interviewers shows your preparation for the interview and your interest in the position. Do not ask about salary. However, you might ask questions like:
    1. What are the organization's greatest challenges in the years ahead?
    2. Why is this position available?
    3. Who will be my supervisor?
    4. What are the opportunities for advancement?

Rehearse the interview. Find someone—spouse, parent, friend—to role play the interview with you. Choose someone you feel comfortable with and who will provide honest feedback to your responses and your interviewing skills. Then assess your strengths and weaknesses and make necessary adjustments. For example, ask your role playing interviewer to tell you if you speak too fast or slowly, too loudly or softly. Ask if you display any nervous habits such as inappropriate facial expressions or folding your arms or slouching. Then adjust these behaviors. You might also consider practicing in front of a mirror or a video camera when you role play. This will help you see the image you are projecting.

- **The Interview**
    Dress for success and to make a positive first impression. If the position you are interviewing for involves an office or business environment, it is appropriate to wear a business suit. If the position consists of a more informal atmosphere; such as a factory or warehouse position; neat, clean, less formal clothes may be appropriate. Also, remember to polish your shoes. Arrive 10 to 15 minutes early. Introduce yourself in a courteous manner. While you wait, read materials about the

company or organization. Shake hands firmly but not crushingly. Obviously, you will feel nervous before and possibly during the interview, but that's a positive sign that your body is telling your brain it is ready for the interview process.

During the interview session, portray a positive image with your body language by standing straight and sitting attentively with both feet on the floor. Let your body language show you are open and receptive by keeping your arms and legs uncrossed. Do not hold a briefcase or purse on your lap. You may choose to carry a notepad to jot down important ideas, but do not focus so much on taking notes that you hamper the smooth flow of the interview process. Avoid chewing gum or sucking on candy or breath mints. Maintain eye contact with the interviewers, and smile and nod at appropriate times. Try to be poised, professional, confident, and genuine. Let the positive traits of your personality help sell you as the right person for the job. Listen attentively to the questions, and offer concise but thorough answers with specific examples to illuminate your responses. Although you have rehearsed responses prior to the interview, try not to let your responses sound rehearsed or canned. Don't become anxious if periods of silence or pauses occur during the interview. Those may be times your interviewers are formulating questions or you are thinking of responses. Remain poised and confident. Refrain from making any negative comments about prior jobs or prior employers. Try to say something positive about your previous employment experiences. And don't look at your watch.

Many employers appreciate seeing concrete evidence of your abilities, either from your academic experiences or from previous employment. A productive method to provide that concrete evidence is creating an employment portfolio. Your portfolio will present a purposeful collection of your work and/or academic experiences that demonstrate your abilities, achievements, accomplishments, and efforts which have prepared you for the position you are interviewing for. The contents of your portfolio should be tailored to your background, experiences, and personality. Before the interview, analyze the job's requirements and skills. Then review the contents of your portfolio and select artifacts that will illustrate your capabilities. Try to be as organized as possible to avoid shuffling papers during the interview.

During the questioning phase of the interview, you can present the contents of your portfolio to concretely show the interviewers what you have accomplished that make you a strong candidate for the position. Remember you might not show everything in your portfolio. Select appropriate items at appropriate junctures of the interview to support your capabilities. Like the entire interview process, it works best if prior to the interview, you rehearse your responses to questions by using your portfolio.

If you use a portfolio, do not hand it over to the interviewers at the beginning of the interview. The employer may choose to look through it rather than give his or her full attention to your verbal responses, or the employer will listen to you and not look at the artifacts you've provided in your portfolio. Also, make copies of your portfolio contents for the interview and keep the originals. Many times employers will ask to keep your portfolio for more thorough analysis following the interview session.

As the interview draws to a close, you may be given the opportunity to ask questions. Be sure the questions are relevant, and don't ask about salary. Reinforce your interest in the position. Take extra copies of your resume and provide a list of references if the employer asks for that information. If another interview is scheduled, be sure to get specific information about it. If this is the concluding interview, you might inquire when a decision on the position will be made and how you will be informed or if you may call to inquire at a certain date and time. Finally, thank the interviewers for the opportunity to interview, and offer your farewell greetings.

FOLLOW-UP

After the interview, jot down notes of significance, such as your initial impressions, things that went well or poorly, and further questions you might ask in the next interview. Evaluate your performance so that you can improve in future interviews. Be sure to write down the names, correctly spelled, and titles of each person who served on the interviewing committee. Then within 24 hours of your interview, write a concise thank you letter to each interviewer. In the thank you letter, express your appreciation for the interview, and indicate your enthusiasm for the position. Clearly inform the interviewers that you want the job and can meet its expectations.

EXAMPLE FOLLOW-UP LETTER

4321 Riverside Drive
North Buena Vista, IA 52066
November 12, 2007

Mr. I. N. Charge
Chief Executive Officer
Smooth Tire Company
10502 Market Rd.
Peosta, IA 52068

Dear Mr. Charge:

I want to thank you for interviewing me yesterday for the controller position in the Accounting Department at Smooth Tire Company. I enjoyed meeting you and the other members of the interviewing committee, and I learned much more about the job requirements and your excellent company.

The interview increased my interest and excitement for the position. I believe my education and professional experience in accounting fit well with the job requirements, and I'm confident I can make major contributions to the continued success of the Smooth Tire Company.

I appreciate the opportunity to interview with you and your committee. If I can answer any further questions, please call me at 563.345.7809. I look forward to knowing your decision in the near future.

Sincerely,

Ann Betteryet

Ann Betteryet

PRACTICE 13D: THANK YOU NOTE. Compose a thank you note for your interviewers that you might be able to adapt for future employment opportunities.

CHAPTER 14

GLOSSARY of Syntactic & Editing FUNdamentals

1. **Adjective** – a word that modifies (describes or limits) a noun or pronoun.

    "It's a <u>beautiful</u> day in the neighborhood."

2. **Adverb** – a word that modifies (describes or limits) a verb, adjective, or another adverb.

    The cow strolled <u>utterly</u> <u>gracefully</u> across the pasture.

3. **Appositive** – a word, phrase, or clause that renames the noun preceding it.

    My brother, the brains in the family, owns five buildings.

4. **Article** – the words *a, an, the*.

5. **Case** – the form, or use of a word, that shows its relationship to other words in a sentence. The three cases are nominative (subject, predicate nominative, direct address), objective (direct object, indirect object, object of preposition), and possessive (ownership, possession).

    <u>I</u> prefer to type the letter. (nominative)
    Kay gave <u>**me**</u> the keys to the car. (objective)
    I gave <u>**my**</u> checkbook to Kay. (possessive)

6. **Clause** – a group of words containing a subject and a predicate and forming a part of a compound or complex sentence. There are two kinds of clauses—independent (main) and dependent (subordinate).

    Dependent (Subordinate) Clause – a clause introduced by a subordinate element. It depends on the rest of the sentence for meaning. A subordinate clause does not express a complete thought and cannot stand alone. It must be attached to the main clause as a part of a sentence. The three kinds of dependent clauses are adverb, adjective, and noun.

He will attend the Hawkeye game <u>if the Hawks promise to win</u>. (adverb)

I am grateful to the student <u>who edited my work</u>. (adjective)

I remember <u>what the boss said</u>. (noun)

Independent (Main) Clause – a clause that is not introduced by a subordinate element. A main clause does not modify. It usually can stand alone as a simple sentence.

<u>Time passes quickly</u> when one is writing.

<u>I knew a fellow</u> who was born in Buenie.

Nonrestrictive Clause – could be omitted without changing the meaning of the sentence and should be surrounded by commas.

Zelmo, <u>who thinks he's high and mighty</u>, fell flat on his face.

Restrictive Clause – could not be omitted from the sentence. Without this clause, a sentence would change in meaning or be misunderstood.

The book <u>that Waldo wrote</u> is selling well.

7. **Complex Sentence** – contains one independent clause and one or more dependent clauses.

After the Cardinals whipped the Cubs, we celebrated.

We agreed with what Homer suggested.

8. **Compound Sentence** – contains two or more independent clauses but no dependent clauses. Clauses may be joined either by a comma + coordinating conjunction (for, and, but, or, nor, yet, so) or by a semi-colon.

Waldo believes everyone, but Hilda needs proof.

Waldo believes everyone; Hilda needs proof.

9. **Compound-Complex Sentence** – contains two or more independent clauses and one or more dependent clauses.

Sally met the Chicago students, who landed at the airport, and she escorted them to NICC.

10. **Gerund Phrase** – a phrase starting with a gerund, the –ing form of a verb. The entire gerund phrase is used like a noun.

Earning a passing grade seemed tougher than I thought.

The strawberry picker was fired for sitting down on the job.

11. **Helping Verbs** – a verb phrase consists of the main verb and one or more helping (auxiliary) verbs. Helping verbs are used with main verbs to express changes in tense, voice, or mood. Note the helping verbs (italicized) in the following examples:

> *has* practiced   *will be* practicing
> *should have* practiced   *should have been* practicing

Common Helping Verbs:

be (am, is, are, was, were, been)	have, has, had	ought
can, could	may, might	shall, will
do, does, did, done	must	should, would

12. **Infinitive Phrase** – a phrase introduced by an infinitive (to + verb). It may be used as a noun, an adjective, or an adverb. Try not to split the *to* from the rest of the verb.

> To refuse the gift seemed foolish. (noun – subject)
> Writing to do was not hard to find. (adjective, adverb)

13. **Number** – refers to singular (one) or plural (two or more).

> Each person should have their coats on. (Number agreement error)
> All people should have their coats on. (Correct)

14. **Participle Phrase** – a phrase starting with a participle. The entire phrase is used like an adjective.

> We watched the instructors figuring our grades.
> Booed beyond belief, the referee forfeited the game.
> Having finished my tax form, I sent in the balance due.

15. **Participle** – a verb form that performs as an adjective or adverb. It may modify a noun or pronoun. It can take an object.

> Gasping, I sucked in air.

16. **Phrase** – a group of related words not expressing a complete thought and without a subject and verb.

> over the river
> through the woods
> to Grandmother's house

17. **Predicate** – the particular word or words that express the action in a sentence. The simple predicate is the verb.

> Harold read the essay to his peer response group.
> Pierre reads, writes, and speaks French fluently.

18. **Prepositional Phrase** – a phrase starting with a preposition and used to modify other words.

    Gloria stepped <u>to the edge</u> of the dock.

19. **Run-on Sentence** – two or more independent clauses run together without proper punctuation.

    > The secretary used the new computer, she bought it down town. (splice)

    > The secretary used the new computer she bought it down town. (fused)

20. **Sentence** – a group of words expressing a complete thought and containing a subject and predicate.

21. **Simple Sentence** – contains one independent clause and no dependent clauses.

    > Margo types 421 words per minute.

22. **Sentence Fragment** – a group of words that does not express a complete thought but is used incorrectly as a sentence. Often a fragment is a dependent clause or a phrase.

    > The pretty girl in the blue dress.

    > Walking into my office yesterday morning.

23. **Subject** – that part of the sentence that does the action (exception: passive voice). The subject can be found by asking, "Who, what did the action?"

    > <u>George Washington</u> chopped down a cherry tree.

    > <u>John</u> and <u>Nancy</u> work in the Writing Center.

24. **Subordinating Conjunction** – a word that introduces a dependent adverb clause. Examples: after, although, as, as if, as though, because, before, if, since, unless, until, when, whenever, where, wherever, while.

25. **Verbal Phrase** – a phrase introduced by a verbal, a word derived from a verb, but used as a noun, adjective, or adverb. The three kinds are participle, gerund, and infinitive.

26. **Voice** – Active voice is preferred over passive voice.

    Active Voice – the subject performs the action of a sentence.

    > The instructor presented a lecture on voice.

    Passive Voice – the subject is the receiver of the action. The word *by* generally indicates passive voice.

    > A lecture on voice was presented by the instructor.

INDEX

Works Cited

Agress, Lynne. *Working With Words in Business and Legal Writing.* Cambridge, MA: Perseus, 2002.

Andersen, Richard, and Helene Hinnis. *The Write Stuff: A Style Manual for Effective Business Writing.* Shawnee Mission, KA: National Press Publications, 1990.

Danziger, Elizabeth. *Get to the Point.* New York: Three Rivers, 2001.

Dickens, Charles. *A Tale of Two Cities.* New York: Signet, 1997.

Elbow, Peter. *Writing With Power.* New York: Oxford UP, 1981.

Forbes, Malcolm. "How to write a business letter." 4 Mar. 2002. 4 Apr. 2006. <http://www.d.umn.edu /cla/faculty/troufs/comp3160/ businessletter.html>. Last Modified 10:00:05 GMT 04 March 2002

Hemingway, Ernest. *New York Journal-American.* 11 July 1961.

King, Stephen. *On Writing—a Memoir of the Craft.* New York: Scribner, 2000.

Kirby, Dan and Tom Liner. *Inside Out: Developmental Strategies for Teaching Writing.* Portsmouth, NH: Boynton/Cook, 1981.

Lannon, John M. *Technical Writing.* New York: HarperCollins, 1994.

Lindemann, Erika. *A Rhetoric for Writing Teachers.* New York: Oxford UP: 1982.

Marius, Richard. *A Writer's Companion.* Boston: McGraw-Hill College, 1999.

Miles, Robert, Marc Bertonasco, and William Karns. *Prose Style, A Guide.* 2nd ed. Englewood Cliffs, NJ: Prentice Hall, 1991.

Murray, Donald. *The Craft of Revision.* Chicago: Holt, Rinehart, Winston, 1991.

National Commission on Writing. *Writing: A Ticket to Work…Or a Ticket Out.* Princeton, NJ: College Board, Sept. 2004.

Perrine, Laurence. "Fifteen Ways to Write Five Hundred Words." *Exploring Language.* Ed. Gary Goshgarian. 5th ed. Glenview, IL: Scott Foresman, 1989.

Provost, Gary. *100 Ways to Improve Your Writing.* New York: Mentor Book, 1985.

Royal, Brandon. *The Little Red Writing Book.* Cincinnati, OH: Writer's Digest Books, 2004.

Scott, Dewitt H. *Secrets of Successful Writing.* San Francisco: Reference Software, 1989.

Shakespeare, William. *Hamlet.* Ed. David Bevington. New York: Bantam, 1988.

Shakespeare, William. *Henry IV, Part I.* Ed. David Bevington. New York: Bantam, 1988.

Strunk, William, Jr., and E.B. White. *The Elements of Style.* 3rd ed. New York: Macmillan, 1979.

Trimble, John R. *Writing With Style.* Englewood Cliffs, NJ: Prentice-Hall, 1975.

Trimmer, Joseph. *Teaching With a Purpose.* 13th ed. Boston: Houghton Mufflin, 2001.

Twain, Mark. *Shoptalk: Learning to Write With Writers.* ed. Donald Murray. Portsmouth, NH: Heinemann, 1990.

Vonnegut, Kurt. "Writing From the Heart." *Chicken Soup for the Writer's Soul.* Ed. Jack Canfield and Mark Victor Hanson. Deerfield Beech, FL: Health Communications, Inc., 2000, 123.

Williams, Joseph. *Style: Ten Lessons in Clarity and Grace.* New York: Longman, 2000.

Younger, Irving. *Persuasive Writing.* Minnetonka, MN: The Professional Education Group, 1990.

Zinsser, William. *Writing to Learn.* New York: Harper & Row, 1988.

PRACTICE EXERCISES ANSWER KEY

Chapter 1   **Getting Down to Business Writing**

PRACTICE 1A: Answers may vary.
  Passage 1:   Three bears—Papa, Mama, and Baby—lived in the forest and enjoyed eating porridge.
  Passage 2:   Don't stretch time breaks. Return to your duties as soon as your scheduled break ends.

Chapter 2   **Plan Your Work. Work Your Plan.**

PRACTICE 2A: Answers will vary.

Chapter 3   **Structure Your correspondence**

PRACTICE 3A: Answers will vary.
PRACTICE 3B: Answers will vary.

Chapter 4   Netiquette

Practice 4A: (Ellen: I returned from New York City and got your email. Thanks. Yes, I understand you want a face to face meeting this week. I cannot meet because my calendar is full. As a matter of fact, I am booked until February. Call for an appointment when you can. See you later. J. L. Brimeyer)

Chapter 5   **Strong Sentence Structure**

PRACTICE 5A: Editing Fragments   Answers may vary.
  1. I have already received five writing awards.
  2. When I was in college, I found writing assignments easy, mostly because of the simple topics which could be completed effortlessly.
  3. Every day I drive 30 miles to work, which becomes a hassle because of the increasing gas prices.
  4. I fear business writing because I struggle with thinking of ideas to write about.
  5. Through this writing seminar, I hope to increase my thinking skills, both in generating ideas and in organizing them.
  6. With the job came many opportunities to write.
  7. I am in the middle of my professional career, a career that I still look forward to.
  8. College professors should require writing in all courses from first year through graduation.
  9. Writing skills are developed with practice and a willingness to learn new editing skills.
  10. Business writing is much different from college, academic writing.

PRACTICE 5B: Editing Run-ons   Answers may vary.
  1. I was recognized as a good writer; however, I had little ambition to write.
  2. Revision has always challenged me. I have always struggled with proper grammar.
  3. I love to write. I find it an interesting and rewarding mental challenge.
  4. College professors told me I have writing talent. I just detest spending so much time on one project.

5.   Sharing my writing with my colleagues scares me. They might find many errors, and I might feel humiliated.
6.   Writing is a skill or craft; it can be learned by everyone.
7.   I took business writing four times in college; unfortunately, it was the same course four times.
8.   I have lived in the same city all my life. I have worked as an insurance agent for ten years.
9.   I have been promoted to Assistant Manager. My supervisors recognized my hard work and positive attitude.
10. My confidence is soaring. I can't wait to write my next business communication.

PRACTICE 5C: Editing Fragments and Run-ons.   Answers will vary.

An eighty-eight-year-old lady could not find her favorite matching necklace and earrings. She searched every inch of her home, but she could not find her treasured jewelry. Her son, a lawyer of some renown, advised his mother to file a claim with her insurance company. After giving her son's advice much thought, she chose to file the claim and called her insurance agent. Obligingly, the service-oriented agent sent the lady the required forms to apply for payment for her lost jewelry.

Upon receipt of the forms, she asked her son to help her fill them out, which he dutifully did. The elderly lady then sent the claims to her agent, who filed them immediately. The process to get the value of the jewels was put in motion. The insurance company sent the lady a check for $1,800 to cover the value of her missing gems.

A few weeks after receiving the check from the insurance company, the lady ran into her insurance agent at a super-market. She informed him that she had found her missing jewels in a box in her garage. The agent told her how pleased he was that she had located her treasured jewelry and asked her to return the $1,800 to the insurance company.

The lady informed the agent that she could not return the money. When she found the jewelry, she felt it would not be fair to keep both jewels and money, so she put the $1,800 into the collection plate at her church.

PRACTICE 5D.   Answers will vary.

Chapter 6   **Smooth and Clear: Parallelism & Misplaced, Dangling Modifiers**

PRACTICE 6A: Parallelism   Answers may vary.
1.   Knowing grammar rules and following them makes writing more orderly and clear.
2.   Harry prefers writing essays to dating girls.
3.   Waldo will attend either NICC or UNI.
4.   Issuing a response would be magnifying the problem.
5.   A grade alert went out to Francis Flunk, Missy Work, and Dorothy Dropped.
6.   The fast pace of society threatens the development and growth of children's personalities.
7.   Both the coach and her assistants received conference honors last season.
8.   Since writing is controlled by purpose, the writer's purpose determines selection and organization of content.

PRACTICE 6B: Parallelism   Answers may vary.
1. …a partridge in a pear tree.   6. …a Mohawk haircut.
2. …also looks intelligent.   7. …also amazed
3. …flood-like rain.   8. …by the easy grading policy.
4. …about her research on leprechauns.   9. …that all employees fill out time cards.
5. …to the sports enthusiast, golf is   10. …and a willingness to learn.
     captivating.

PRACTICE 6C: Misplaced Modifiers   Answers may vary.
1. The Peosta police reported two ransacked college dorms.
2. In Iowa, a farmer owned a calf born with two heads,
3. The college's cafeteria serves students beverages in little cans.
4. A new computer, which has caused a lot of trouble, was donated to the Human Resources Department.
5. For Christmas, Marissa's godfather Elmo gave her a new doll called "Little Cuddles."
6. The dog distracted Gladys, who was working on her letter.
7. The swerving semi missed the fawn that was standing in the middle of the highway.
8. For his library, Professor Wright bought a composition book that costs $12.50.

PRACTICE 6D: Dangling Modifiers   Answers will vary.
1. As Lily lay on the hammock for three hours, the sun's rays grew hotter and hotter.
2. After the dentist pulled my three teeth, my gums felt sore.
3. When I was four-years-old, my mother gave birth to my younger brother.
4. As Mary prepares this letter, she will need to create a detailed outline.
5. As the mail carrier came up the front walk, she saw the mailbox located near the front door.
6. After spending all night in the library, I was exhausted.
7. When I was ten-years-old, my family took a vacation to the Grand Titans.
8. While Hilda visited with her friends, the topic of employment came up.

PRACTICE 6E: Squinting Modifiers   Answers will vary.
1. I told only the police officer what I had seen.
2. I ate almost the whole pie.
3. Hilda said the manager belched six times during the meeting.
4. Frequently my daughter was advised to submit her tax forms.
5. Jack was told to register for next semester's classes the next day.

PRACTICE 6F: Misplaced, Dangling, Squinting Modifiers   Answers will vary.
1. The student with misplaced modifiers was referred to the Writing Center.
2. Tomorrow Tom will make plans to publish his writing.
3. When I was four-years-old, my mother took me to swimming lessons.
4. While Maggie was dressing for the winter formal, the doorbell rang.
5. Zelmo was often told to eliminate squinting modifiers.
6. Kerry Wood soaked his strained arm in ice.
7. As Fred drove down the winding road, he saw that a duck and her duckling had halted traffic for five minutes.
8. On the way to work, Tom saw the swans swimming in the lake.
9. As Liz watched the evening news, her pet hamster escaped from its cage.
10. As I look back through 45 years, I recall many people who influenced my life.

Chapter 7   Conciseness /Cut the Deadwood

PRACTICE 7A: Conciseness   Answers may vary.

1. since or because	7. ended	12. passes	17. descend
2. now	8. agree	13. replied	18. calmed myself
3. same spot	9. few	14. return	19. green
4. raised	10. huddled	15. control	20. obviously
5. finished	11. merge	16. sinks	21. smile
6. gather			

PRACTICE 7B: Conciseness

Answers may vary.

1. We checked in

11. The inside of my truck looks messy.

2. I started the car

12. Cindy's father's resignation shocked everyone.

3. I feared

13. I have some strange luck.

4. I sprinted

14. I ran down the stairs faster than I have ever moved before.

5. I told her everything

6. I wondered…

15. I lost compassion for the snake.

16. I didn't sleep much last night.

7. They resented each other.

17. We lined up in the cafeteria to be congratulated by everyone.

8. My brother replied…

18. Some Americans don't mind illegal immigrants entering this country.

19. At a young age, I was taught to respect guns.

9. Three and four days passed

20. I am returning to school to make a better life for my family and me.

10. It unites everyone.

PRACTICE 7C: Conciseness   Answers will vary.

1. Evidently some employees submitted their business correspondence early for added vacation days. (12)
2. After looking everywhere for a research article on Medicare, the insurance agent copied information from his insurance manual. (18)
3. Our Seattle vacation was hampered by daily rain. (8)
4. From our seats behind home plate at Wrigley Field, we could judge the home plate umpire's calls. (17)
5. Employees complain that all supervisors evaluate personnel on the same day. (11)

Chapter 8   **Say What You Mean. Mean What You Say.**

PRACTICE 8A: Be Specific   Answers will vary.

PRACTICE 8B: Be Specific   Answers will vary.

PRACTICE 8C: Be Specific   Answers will vary.

1. Fourteen-year-old Tom Smith read *Sports Illustrated* until 11:30 Thursday night.
2. Mac placed his knife in his dad's Ford Apache.
3. The composition instructor discussed Wilfred's grade with him.
4. The Jones family visited Chicago, ate at Hardy,s, and attended the Decayed Corpses' concert.
5. My pet gopher escaped this morning, but Fran Find, a restaurant owner on Jackson Street, found her at Comiskey Park.
6. Gigi Chord attends NICC, works at the Red Roof Diner, and plays spoons in the Four Stumps Band.
7. According to the *NICC Herald*, English Instructor Jim Brimeyer has written *You've Gotta Have Heart—in Your WRITING*, a composition textbook.
8. Randy Rush quickly vaulted into his 1978 Chevy and raced through the NICC parking lot toward the exit.

WORD USAGE

1. **accept** – verb "to receive";   **except** – preposition "excluding"

We **accept** your invitation.

If you **accept** his first semester's grades, he has accumulated a good grade point.

My grades appear satisfactory in every course **except** physics.

2. **affect** – verb "to influence, to cause";   **effect** – noun "result"
   ("tip" – action = **verb** = affect)
   How did the defeat **affect** the team?
   Everyone felt the **effect** of the strike.

3. **all right** & **a lot** – always spelled as two words, not "alright, a lot."

4. **alumna**=singular female; **alumnae**=plural females; **alumnus**=singular male; **alumni**=plural males or both genders.
   My wife Kay is an **alumna** of Clarke College.
   Her husband Jim is an **alumnus** of Loras College.
   Mark and Mary are **alumni** of the University of Dubuque.

5. **amount** – use with a singular words;   **number** – use with a plural word.
   She always carried a small **amount** of money.
   The Bears' line displays a tremendous **amount** of power.
   A **number** of fumbles occurred during the second quarter.
   He held a **number** of coins in his hand.

6. **although** – subordinating conjunction;   **however** – adverb;
   introduces a dependent clause.   meaning "on the other hand" or "by contrast."
   Although it was 10 degrees below zero, I didn't feel a thing.
   It was 10 degrees below zero; **however**, I didn't feel a thing.

7. **bad** – adjective (modifies noun or pronoun);   **badly** - adverb or pronoun); (modifies verb, adjective, adverb)
   The Cubs play **badly**.
   The stockyards smell **bad**.

8. **beside** – "by the side of" someone or something;   **besides** – adv. "in addition to" or prep. "except"
   Along came a spider and sat down **beside** her.
   He owned nothing **besides** his good name.
   He received a medal and five dollars **besides**.

9. **between** – use with two;   **among** – use with more than two.
   The ball was passed **between** Phil and you.
   We earned two dollars **among** the five of us.

10. **borrow** – "to get with the intention of returning"   **lend** – "to give someone something you expect to get back"
    I **borrowed** some money from my father.
    Lisa didn't want to **lend** me any of her clothes.

11. **bring** – denotes motion toward a place   **take** – denotes motion away from a place
    Bring my business letter here.
    Take my business letter there.

12. **can**–expresses ability;   **may**–expresses permission or possibility
    May I accompany you to the dance?
    Can you type 3,000 words per minute?

13. **could of, should of, would of** – of is not a verb.
    correct = **could have, should have, would have**
    The composition instructor should of given us more work.
    The composition instructor should **have** given us more work.

14. **due to** or **due to the fact that** - use <u>since</u>, <u>because</u>, or <u>because of</u>, unless **due** functions as predicate adjective.

        Nonstandard: Due to the fact that we have so much rain, the game is cancelled.

        Correct: **Because** we have so much rain, the game is cancelled.

15. **fewer** – use with a plural word;   **less** – use with a singular word.

        I encounter **<u>fewer</u>** health problems than I did 10 years ago.

        I save **<u>less</u>** money than I did 10 years ago.

16. **good** – adjective, modifies a noun   **well** – adverb ("perform an action capably" or adjective – "in good health); ("satisfactory")

        The Cardinals played **<u>well</u>** against the Cubs.

        Violet sang **<u>well</u>** in the concert.

        Herman does not feel **<u>well</u>** after eating four pizzas.

        Otto appears to be in **<u>good</u>** health.

        Ellen looks **<u>good</u>** in that new, blue dress.

        His clothes never fit him **<u>well</u>**.

17. **imply** – "to suggest something";   **infer** – "to interpret, to conclude" from.

        A writer or speaker **<u>implies</u>** to a reader or listener.

        A reader or listener **<u>infers</u>** from a writer or speaker.

18. **in** – "located within";   **into** – "from the outside into"

        We were all gathered **<u>in</u>** my grandparents' living room.

        Joe just walked **<u>into</u>** my office.

19. **irregardless** –drop **IR**–should be regardless.

        <u>Regardless</u> of the score, our team won.

20. **it's** – "it is";   **its** – possessive

        Dubuque proudly boasts of **<u>its</u>** hills.

        <u>It's</u> not too late.

        <u>It's</u> a long way to Tipperary.

        The dog chewed on **<u>its</u>** bone.

21. **lay** – "put or place" (lay, laying, laid, laid);   **lie** –"rest or recline" (lie, lying, lay, lain)

        Last night Homer **<u>lay</u>** in his bed all night.

        Waldo **<u>laid</u>** his gun on the table.

        <u>Lay</u> the dish on the counter.

        I plan to **<u>lie</u>** in the sun this afternoon.

22. **leave** – "to go away from";   **let** – "to allow or permit"

        I am **<u>leaving</u>** my past life behind.

        I will **<u>let</u>** him have my answer soon.

        We will **<u>leave</u>** if you **<u>let</u>** us.

23. **like** – preposition, introduces a phrase;   **as** or **as if** – subordinating conjunction introduces a clause.

        She looks **<u>like</u>** a queen.

        She does **<u>as</u>** she wishes.

24. **principal**—(noun or adjective) noun: person in a high position or important role; adjective: means "chief" or "most important." Also, a sum of money lent or borrowed.   **principle**—(only a noun) guiding rule or fundamental truth

        Kay provides the **<u>principal</u>** income in our family.

        The **<u>principal</u>** of your high school acts like your "pal."

        It opposed his **<u>principles</u>** to give easy grades.

        I pay the **<u>principal</u>** and interest on my homeowner's loan.

25. **rise** – "to go up" (rise, rose, risen);   **raise**–"to force something up" (raise, raised, raised)

>The sun is **rising** in the sky.
>The farmer **raised** two chickens and two daughters.

26. **set** – "to put or place";   **sit** – "to seat yourself"

>Please **sit** down.
>Please **set** your glass down.

27. **than** – used in comparisons;   **then** – adverb of time

>Hilda seems stronger **than** Waldo.
>She ate breakfast and **then** brushed her teeth.
>**Then** the waiter handed us the bill.
>Our house costs more **than** theirs.

28. **double negative** – **can't hardly, can't scarcely** (hardly and scarcely are negatives when combined with <u>not</u>), **can't help but; no, nothing, none** combined with **not.**

Examples of Nonstandard Usage:

>I can't hardly tell the difference between this year's cars and last year's.
>There wasn't scarcely enough food for everyone.
>Haven't you no ticket?
>I can't help but admire his courage.
>She hasn't nothing to do.
>He didn't give me none.

Corrected Nonstandard Usage:

>I can hardly tell the difference between this year's cars and last year's.
>There wasn't enough food for everyone.
>Have you no ticket?
>I admire his courage.
>She has nothing to do. OR She hasn't anything to do.
>He didn't give me any.

PRACTICE 8D: Word Usage   (Some answers may vary.)

1. fewer	10. accepted	19. C
2. affect	11. number	20. as
3. C	12. C	21. let
4. C	13. C	22. Take
5. among	14. number	23. number
6. C	15. C	24. affected
7. have	16. lending	25. can hardly
8. bring	17. let	
9. fewer	18. implied	

PRACTICE 8E: Word Usage   (Some answers may vary.)

1. have	6. C	11. delete had	16. lying
2. Let	7. anything	12. lain	17. lie
3. Besides	8. well	13. well	18. well
4. as if	9. take	14. lay	19. fewer
5. fewer	10. Because of	15. rising	

Chapter 9   Action Verbs, Active Voice, Avoiding Shifts

PRACTICE 8A: Weak Verbs vs. Helping Verbs

Helping Verbs   Main Verbs   Helping Verbs   MainVerbs

1. had	finished	6. Do	believe
2. must have been	planning	7. would have	understood
3. should have	asked	8. would have	extended
4.	felt	9. would	go
5.	approached	10. will	know

PRACTICE 9B: Style-Verb Strength   Answers may vary.
1. I, Robin Goodfellow, was born on January, 12, 1984, at Story County Hospital.
2. I worry a little about my career choice, but anything worthwhile presents challenges.
3. After my lay-off, I knew I would return to school. I graduated 30 years ago, and my children now attend college.
4. My parents, Herman and Hilda, gave each of my brothers names that start with "H."
5. My sister, an eleven-year-old fourth grader, attends Romper Room School.
6. I am enrolled in the AA program, a big change from high school.
7. I explored a lot of open fields and wild timber there.
8. As a little girl, I read *Grimm's Fairy Tales.*
9. Until recently, my parents, Mickey and Minnie Mouse, have lived in Disneyland.
10. I could publish all of my adventures.

PRACTICE 9C: Style-Verb Strength   Answers will vary.

PRACTICE 9D: Passive—Active Voice   Answers will vary.
1. All composition students must meet the expectations explained in the course syllabus.
2. Each employee has processed business letters and will share them at the next staff meeting.
3. Over the years, many college basketball players used ankle-supported basketball shoes.
4. The college's medical staff had given flu shots to the majority of the first year class.
5. Most good writers prefer active voice sentences over passive voice sentences.

PRACTICE 9E: Passive—Active Voice   Answers will vary.
In 1874, Robert Frost was born in San Francisco. After his father's death, his mother raised him in New England. Frost attended both Dartmouth and Harvard, but he did not graduate from college. Frost loved farming and rural New England life, and his poetry addresses these subjects. Frost married Elinor White, and he moved his family to England in 1912 to farm and write. In 1913, Englishman David Nutt published Frost's first book, *A Boy's Will.* Two years later the Frost family returned to New England, and Americans heralded Frost as a major poet. Frost won the Pulitzer Prize four times. In 1961, President John F. Kennedy invited Frost to read the poem "The Gift Outright" at the Presidential Inauguration. Robert Frost died in 1963, but his poetry lives prominently in American literature.

PRACTICE 9F: Unnecessary Shifts   Answers will vary.
1. The President of the College read a statement to the students but refused to respond to any questions.
2. If first year college students expect to earn good grades, they need to organize their time and study habits consistently.
3. Students should not expect to rely on their parents for all their financial support because they will need to support themselves as adults.
4. When they feel the flu coming on, students should rest and drink plenty of fluids.
5. When we go to Florida for spring break, we will visit the beach for sun and fun.
6. The wide receiver caught the pass and weaved his way through three defenders toward the end zone.

7. We left for the library at 11 o'clock, and on the way, we ate a sub-sandwich at the snack bar.
8. Drama enthusiasts should watch Mel Gibson's portrayal of Hamlet.
9. The supervisor reads the first peer's essay and forty-five minutes later reads the third letter.
10. The manager read the report and then wrote the response.

PRACTICE 9G: Unnecessary Shifts   Answers will vary.

Henry David Thoreau lived from 1817 to 1862 around Concord, Massachusetts. Thoreau's father, a pencil maker, provided him with a Harvard education. For two years, Ralph Waldo Emerson, his long-time friend, housed Thoreau. At age 28, Thoreau built a small cabin on the shore of Walden Pond near Concord. Thoreau lived there for two years, and he published his famous book *Walden* in 1854. The book described the natural charms of the woods. American thinkers recognized how much Thoreau's comments on simple living and deep thinking contributed to 19th century American thought. Although Thoreau did not urge readers to imitate his example of solitary living, many readers of *Walden* followed its message.

Chapter 10   **"Let's Come to Agreement"**

PRACTICE 10A: SV Agreement:

1. is	7. is	12. types	18. seems	24. flies
2. rides	8. needs	13. have	19. is	
3. are	9. is	14. are	20. is	
4. was	10. are	15. is	21. have	
5. was		16. are	22. sings	
6. is	11. is	17. is	23. need	

PRACTICE 10B: SV Agreement

1. has	5. C	9. C	13. C
2. are	6. was	10. change	14. locks
3. C	7. are	11. is	15. are
4. are	8. was	12. Does	

PRACTICE 10C: SV Agreement   Answers will vary.

PRACTICE 10D: Pron-Antecedent Agreement

1. they	3. his	5. they	7. its	9. its
2. her	4. their	6. their	8. their	10. their

PRACTICE 10E: Pron-Antecedent Agreement

1. Writers or (his or her)	5. their	8. its
2. their	6. their	9. C
3. C	7. his/her	10. their
4. his/her		

PRACTICE 10F: Answers will vary.

Chapter 11   **Adjective-Adverb & Pronoun Usage**

PRACTICE 11A: Modifiers

1. softly	5. quickly	9. sweet
2. really	6. wonderful	10. recently

3. immensely   7. delicious, horrible
4. heartily, correctly   8. silent, still

PRACTICE 11B: Modifiers
1. looked happily   5. loudly, quickly   9. unexpectedly, really quietly
2. softly   6. correctly, smooth   10. frightful, delightful
3. quickly, quietly   7. odd, suddenly
4. slowly   8. cautiously, calm

PRACTICE 11C: Modifiers
1. really   4. well   7. slowly, surely
2. surely   5. easily   8. well
3. really well 6. well, really good

PRACTICE 11D: Degrees
1. smarter   2. fastest   3. more   4. most

PRACTICE 11E: Modifiers
1. well   4. C   7. C   10. sharply
2. really quickly   5. surely, sturdily 8. quickly
3. really well   6. really   9. C

PRACTICE 11F: Modifiers
1. unusually   4. really slowly   7. well   10. loudly and clearly
2. oddly   5. C   8. carefully   11. good
3. C   6. surely smells good   9. best

Incorrect Pronoun Usage
1. He and I   12. Mary and he   3. you and she   4. David and I

PRACTICE 11G: Nominative Case
1. she   4. he   7. he   10. She and I   13. I
2. she   5. she   8. he   11. they   14. he
3. he   6. I   9. he   12. he   15. she

PRACTICE 11H: Objective Case
1. me   4. her   7. her   10. them   13. me
2. her   5. her   8. me   11. me   14. him
3. him and her   6. him   9. her   12. him   15. him

PRACTICE 11I: Pronouns
1. me   3. her   5. her   7. We   9. me
2. C   4. He   6. C   8. us   10. himself

PRACTICE 11J: Who/Whom
1. Who   3. Whom   5. who   7. who   9. whoever
2. who   4. Who   6. whom 8. whomever   10. Whom

PRACTICE 11K: All Pronoun Usage
1. who   4. him   7. her   10. they
2. I   5. We   8. who   11. them
3. they   6. C   9. she   12. she

PRACTICE 11L: All Pronoun Usage

1. We	4. C	7. who	10. me
2. They	5. me	8. C	11. he
3. we	6. his	9. they	12. her

Chapter 12   **Good Mechanics**

COMMA PRACTICE 12A:

1. Oh, I almost forgot today's seminar.
2. In my opinion, commas can confuse even the best writers.
3. Expecting the worst, we planned for the project.
4. Tripped in the hallway by Ralph, Jim was carried to the doctor's office.
5. Before the half, the Packers jogged into the locker room.
6. After the game ended, the Hawks had won again.
7. Because writing is challenging, I must put forth good effort.
8. Harry, are you chilly on top?
9. Typing for only ten minutes, Hilda finished the forty-five page essay.
10. If students study hard, they usually do well in college.
11. Having studied for only ten minutes, Waldo approached the quiz apprehensively.
12. While the Cubs lose, the Cardinals continue to win.

COMMA PRACTICE 12B: Answers will vary

COMMA PRACTICE 12C: Place commas in the following sentences.

1. Kay, too, teaches elementary students.
2. Shakespeare, my favorite dramatist, wrote 37 wonderful plays.
3. Yes, Herman, you have a bad case of halitosis.
4. Bob Hope, a terrific comedian, instilled laughter into the hearts of most Americans.
5. Early computers, large and immobile, have been replaced by smaller models.
6. Kay, my lovely wife, teaches third grade.
7. Mr. Ed, who talked like a human, ate like a horse.
8. Buenie, where I was raised, looks like a pimple on the large cheek of Iowa.
9. My dad, whom I greatly respected, placed a fair and valid curfew on his sons.
10. My brother, the thinker in the family, earns more money than I.
11. Karen Morris, who was offered four scholarships, will attend NICC this fall.
12. The computer, working quickly and accurately, processed useful information.

COMMA PRACTICE 12D: Answers will vary.

COMMA PRACTICE 12E: Answers will vary.

1. I visualize a quiet, relaxing, pleasant, and peaceful office.
2. She liked the manager when he was kind, when he was patient, and when he left the class.
3. Our computer expert acted fairly smart, but sometimes he suffered from an e-mail virus.
4. The eighty-year-old couple were married, and they spent their honeymoon on the mountain slopes of Vail.
5. I need to earn some extra money; therefore, I teach some extra classes.
6. The instructor stumbled into the classroom, bumped into the desk, kicked a chair, and laughed in relief.
7. Most of us loved the class, but Zeke considered it boring.
8. We worked on the letter for hours and then handed it to the supervisor.

9. I put in long hours at my job, yet I could do even more.
10. Joe does not fear snakes, nor do turtles frighten him.
11. You must honor the office policies or suffer the consequences.

PRACTICE 12F: Answers will vary.

PRACTICE 12G: Answers will vary

PRACTICE 12H: Comma Usage

1 - introductory word	4 – interrupting word	7 – intertwining series
2 - introductory phrase	5 – interrupting phrase	8 – compound sent.
3 – introductory clause	6 – interrupting clause	9 – date or address

Professor I.M. Snoring had spent countless hours researching his area of
5
expertise, advanced microscopic photosynthesis. He was planning a lecture for his 8 AM
2
class the following Monday. After many hours in the library, Professor Snoring had
8
accumulated a large stack of notes. He then organized them in outline form, and he placed
them in a three-ring binder. The professor was pleased with his work and anxiously awaited
the opportunity to share his expertise with his class.
3
When the night before the lecture arrived, Professor Snoring stayed up late into
2
the evening reviewing his notes. After about five hours of study, he grew tired and
2   8
decided to get some rest. At 6:30 AM, he heard his alarm go off, and he immediately
7   7
jumped out of bed. He brushed his teeth, put on his best sweater, and ate his Corn Flakes.
2
In an eager frame of mind, he hopped on his Honda motorcycle and headed for his office.
3
Although the traffic slowed him a bit, Professor Snoring arrived at the campus in
7   7
good time, found a spot close to his office, and tied his motorcycle to a tree. He briskly
2
walked to his office and unlocked the door. On the floor, he found a letter from his
6   9   9   9/6   9
brother Waldo, who lived at 1032 High Lane, Filmore, Iowa, which was dated May 1,
6   6
2003. Waldo, who was born three years before the professor, farmed 380 acres just off
2   9   9
Highway 151. In the letter, Waldo said he was planning a vacation trip to Millville, Iowa,
and hoped the professor would join him. Professor Snoring decided to respond to the request at a
later time.
Then Professor Snoring left for his eagerly anticipated 8 AM lecture. The students
groggily entered the lecture hall after their long weekend. The professor began his lecture
8
as late-comers continued to straggle in one by one, but that did not derail the professor's
2
speech. After one hour and fourteen minutes of non-stop lecture, the professor finally looked up
from his notes to find numerous listeners fast asleep. The professor became

7   7   7   dialogue 4
undone, halted his lecture, picked out a student in the back of the room, and said, "Say,
  4   6   dialogue
John, would you please wake up that student, who is sleeping in the seat next to you?"
              2   dialogue   5
        In reply, the startled John stammered, "You wake him up yourself, Professor Snoring.
You put him to sleep."

PRACTICE 12I: OVERALL PRACTICE: Answers will vary.

PRACTICE 12J: Apostrophes

a. today	today's assignments	b. boss	boss's tirade
c. job	job's pressures	d. workers	workers' duties
e. attorney	attorney's fees	f. attorneys	attorneys' parking lot
g. men	men's basketball league	h. anybody	anybody's guess

PRACTICE 12K: Apostrophes

a. Stephen King's and John Grisham's novels

b. Tom, Dick, and Harry's project

c. four –s's and four –i's in Mississippi

d. Rodgers and Hammerstein's *The King and I*

e. Tom's, Dick's, and Harry's bikes (each own a bike)

f. It's time for the secretarial staff to take its coffee break.

g. Don't snore.

PRACTICE 12L: Apostrophes

1. Women's lib grows stronger because of its forceful position.
2. The girls' choir will sing for the men's glee club.
3. We've won the clients' confidence.
4. Before Friday's rain, Charley's goat ate eight acres of grass and felt an ache in its stomach.
5. My mother-in-law's cooking has become famous in three states.
6. When you're editing your drafts, check carefully to dot your i's and cross your t's.

PRACTICE 12M: Apostrophes

The students' essays show good use of the writing process. Student writers' revision strategies have been used effectively. Everyone's focus on improving his or her writing style is encouraging. Each student's editing is also improving. Strunk and White's book, *Elements of Style*, seems to be helping all the writers' knowledge of style. People from miles around Peosta will flock to read the students' wonderful writings.

Chapter 13   Job Seeking Skills

PRACTICE 13A: Answers will vary.

PRACTICE 13B: Answers will vary.

PRACTICE 13C: Answers will vary.

PRACTICE 13D: Answers will vary.

LaVergne, TN USA
09 April 2010
178734LV00004B/6/P